How to: Tell Your LGBTQ+ Story

Recognising, writing, and marketing your personal queer life experiences.

David Ledain

This edition was published in Great Britain 2021

Copyright © David Ledain 2021

David Ledain has asserted his right under the Copyright, Design and Patents Act 1988 to be identified as the author of this book.

All rights reserved. No part of this publication may be reproduced, stored in a retrieval system, or transmitted, in any form or by any means, without the prior written permission of the publisher.

ISBN-978-1-5272-9824-8

Published by: Gay Stardust Publishing

Cover design by: Black Jazz Design

For Andy Goss-Durant

1959 – 2019

A friend I ran out of time to tell my story to.

Also by David Ledain:

Having Gay Sex – A Guide to Male Homosexual Sex
This Forbidden Fruit – Male Homosexuality: A Culture & History Guide
Gay Dad – Ten True Stories of Divorced Gay Men With Kids, Living in the UK Today

You can follow David on Facebook & Twitter
@DavidLedain

You can also very easily leave a review for
How to: Tell Your LGBTQ+ Story here:
www.amazon.co.uk/howtotellyourlgbtq+story/createreview

Contents

About This Book 9
Introduction 12

Part One: Becoming A Writer 17

1 Telling their Story: David Ledain 19
   1.1 Fiction v Non-Fiction 23
   1.2 Using A Penname 27
2 Publishers And Agents 31
   2.1 Partnership Publishing 34
   2.2 Book Distribution 37
   2.3 Amazon 39
   2.4 IngramSpark 42
3 Telling their Story: Gary H. James 44
4 Building Blocks 48
   4.1 Time 48
   4.1.1 Planning The Road Ahead 50
   4.2 Invest In Your Education 53
   4.3 Find Fellow Authors 54
   4.3.1 Set Up A Writers' Group 55
5 Getting Expert Help 59
   5.1 Planning Your Budget 60
   5.1.1 Crowdfunding 65
6 What Is Stopping You? 69
   6.1 Am I Expert Enough? 73
   6.2 Mental Health 76
7 Telling their Story: Gideon E. Wood 79

Part Two: Your Book 85

8 Structuring And Researching Your Book 87
   8.1 Conducting Interviews 92
   8.2 Finding Your Voice 97
9 Telling their Story: Curtis Chin 99

10 Seven Basic Storyline Plots	104
10.1 Using Your Diaries	105
11 Editors, Editing And Proofreading	109
11.1 Preliminary And End Matter	113
11.2 Back-of-Book Blurb	122
12 Telling their Story: Nick Taylor	124
13 Cover Design	130
14 Formatting And Uploading Your Book	133
15 Telling their Story: JD Glass	138

Part Three: Marketing   141

16 Make A Plan	143
16.1 Get Leverage In Your Community	147
16.2 Writing Competitions	148
16.3 The Email Mailing List	149
16.4 Defining Your Typical Customer	151
16.5 Create An Elevator Pitch	153
16.6 Write A Press Release	155
17 Telling their Story: Frederic Davies	161
18 Before You Press Publish	167
18.1 Tips For Holding A Launch Party	170
18.2 Post Launch	173
18.3 Merchandise	175
18.4 Virtual Blog Tours	177
18.5 Reviews	180
19 Telling their Story: Gireesh	182
20 Presenting You, The Author	188
20.1 Podcasts	193
20.2 Radio	195
20.3 Giving A Talk	200
21 Websites/Blogs	205
21.1 What Is The Difference Between .co.uk And .com?	210
22 Telling their Story: Helen Dale	213
23 Social Media	219

23.1 Facebook	220
23.2 Facebook Advertising	225
23.3 Twitter	228
23.4 Hashtags – What Are They And How To Use Them?	231
23.5 Copyright	232
23.6 Other Social Media	233
24 Telling their Story: Ian Elmslie	237
25 Frequently Asked Questions	240
Epilogue	249
Helpful Links	251
Acknowledgements	253

About This Book

How To: Tell Your LGBTQ+ Story is an authentic account of my journey through self-publishing: my dreams, my goals, the truths and myths I've discovered along the way, and how best to use what I've learned in order to market and sell books. I believe this knowledge will help you too.

I do not profess to be a self-publishing guru. There are other ways to self-publish and promote your book. However, the methods and guidance I describe in the following pages are specifically aimed at helping and encouraging LGBTQ+ people who have an urge to write and self-publish their own life experiences. I will not up-sell further marketing materials to you, or expensive online courses.

I have written this book for you to use in your own way, and in your own time.

Today is a time like no other in which LGBTQ+ people are finding their voices and are being listened to. The more our stories are read and heard, the more diverse ways of living will become the norm. I believe passionately in the power of good that can come from this, and it is just as vital to us as individuals as it is to those within our immediate circles, and wider society.

In writing this book I was especially keen to talk to other LGBTQ+ people who have written and published their life stories, to get a different perspective and to demonstrate the importance of shared personal experiences. Here you will read the true-life stories of LGBTQ+ people from diverse cultures and backgrounds, whose lives have taken different paths and who have experienced different coming out stories. Each of them is unique and told in their own words.

I am immensely grateful to them all for their honesty and involvement. My hope is that these inspirational stories, together with the practical information on self-publishing, will aid and inspire all LGBTQ+ people to write and self-publish their stories too.

It is said that we all carry an unwritten book inside us. *How To: Tell Your LGBTQ+ Story* **will help you unlock that potential.**

You may wish to realise a long-held dream of holding in your hands, that book you have written, or you might have grander plans to become a full-time writer, creating an income through your writing. There is no golden ticket enclosed, but I do believe that if you have the desire to share your story with others, a love of writing, and are not sure how to achieve that, then this book is for you.

Before you delve in, full of excitement to get started, one small word of advice; writing and publishing a book is not easy, and traditional publishing is nigh-on impossible to get into for the unknown writer. I believe in a hybrid version of publishing, of diversification, and connectivity. There is no right or wrong way to go about it, whatever works for you is fine. Fundamentally, whichever path you take to make a success of your writing, whether that inevitably leads to the traditional route, or via self-publishing, it will require a lot of hard work and dedication. Both of which you have. Your enthusiasm has already drawn you to this book, and you will learn a lot of practical advice from it.

This is not a book about creative writing. You will not find within these pages chapters on how to write, and you won't be bombarded with the minutia of unnecessary button-pressing detail. Although self-publishing processes are covered, of course, there are plenty of resources elsewhere that can give you as much detailed technical information as you require. I *will* share a secret with you though: the plain truth of what I have discovered: that what people are interested in, and what sells, are the personal experiences, and real-life stories of other people. It is *you*, and what *you* have been through in *your* life that people will be fascinated by, and the reason for this is that we look to others as roles models to validate and better ourselves. We crave that association of the shared experience and for LGBTQ+ people the desire to find comparable stories to our own is even more crucial. People will search for your book because its topic will resonate with them. It will tell a story that can only be by you, and by telling that story, you will aid others to find their voices too. Writing your book will also help you to understand who you are.

Your book, and your knowledge, can and will make a positive difference to someone's life. So, if you want your words to touch just one person's soul, write them down, and together we will *Tell Your LGBTQ+ Story*.

David Ledain

Introduction

A lot of people who read how-to books have all the best intentions of progressing their idea towards an end result, to see something they have created cross the finish line. But what stops a lot of people, and what they need to get there, is the determination to reach that very goal.

Whether it be writing, running, or playing the guitar proficiently, for any pastime or interest to have sustainability and momentum to help it grow, it must be something that you are truly passionate about. Having such enthusiasm and fervour for something means that you have a deep connection to it. Others might call it a madness, but whatever your thing is, it will tick all your boxes.

You might also think that it's far too late for you, that there are so many books published every day, that the very idea of putting a book that you've written onto the market fills you with dread, made worse by pessimistic voices inside your head telling you that nobody is going to be interested in *your* story.

This is not true. People are interested, and they will be interested in your story.

What can often stop people from taking their passion for writing to that next level, to produce a book, is that rather than do it themselves, they would actually prefer for someone else to do all the things for them they have read and learned about.

There is no shame in being that romantic, starry-eyed idealist who dreams of gliding along a creative path where all the nitty-gritty stuff just happens to get done miraculously. Don't be fooled, however, by this myth of the soft-focused world we imagine the likes of Jane Austen or the Brontë sisters inhabiting. It does not, and never did, exist in real life. In their day, there were insurmountable difficulties for women to get their work published. It didn't just *happen* for them either, and as LGBTQ+ writers we can sympathise with discrimination, and failure to be noticed. Even today, traditionally published, mainstream authors still have to dedicate inordinate amounts of time and energy in getting themselves recognised, doing a lot of their own marketing and promoting. It goes without saying that publishers and agents alike expect their authors to have long email lists and active social media accounts, with thousands of followers hanging on their every post, even before their manuscript hits the publisher's desk.

How do we begin to climb that seemingly impossible publishing mountain?

The vast potential and global reach of the internet is part of the empowering solution at our disposal. There has quite simply never been a time in history that allows ordinary people, without an inheritance or patronage, the scope, and opportunity to realise their creativity in the way the internet can today. Writers, musicians, painters and filmmakers all use the Web and social media networks to get their work out to their audiences, and they do this without going insane, or slipping into the cliché of the angst artist/writer scratching away in a lonely garret, penniless, and starving. With a little initiative, and the ability to surf millions of websites, forums, groups, and social media platforms, spaces can easily be found where LGBTQ+ writers can connect with like-minded people who support each other. You can chat, learn, and make meaningful connections, all for free, you just need to look for your tribe.

There isn't a single person who has not gone through some sort of adversity in their lives, and for LGBTQ+ people those experiences are often more pronounced, have added significance, and are frequently life changing. And while equality has given the LGBTQ+ community much to celebrate over the past twenty years, in that divergence of gay culture into the mainstream, we are in danger of losing our self-identity, and we face the risk of being ignored altogether.

It is just as important today, as it always has been, that we tell our stories.

We humans are a resilient species, and we have mechanisms that aid us to bounce back from hardship and trauma, and one of the most enduring and altruistic of these is the act of sharing our experiences and personal stories with others. Ever since people gathered in groups around a fire, they would sit and tell tales, pass on fables, parables and legends, in order to make sense of their world. And still this tradition lives on in storytelling and confessionals swapped around the campfire, at the hearth or bedside, or in rooms with listening audiences. The community that storytelling evokes is especially true for LGBTQ+ people, who often find themselves forced to hide away for many years in the closet and in shame.

Writing our stories gives us purpose as well as enabling us to draw a line under a traumatic past. Emotive, autobiographical storytelling not only helps us to own our true selves, but also to use our journeys in a way that helps others on a similar path. Likewise, it is well known that sharing ourselves, by revealing the personal and intimate details of our life experiences, can have a positive impact on our own psychological, as well as physical, health. It can be both a cleansing experience and a way of dispelling demons.

Writing your book will not be the hardest thing you've had to do in your life, but doing anything well, with meaning and authenticity is never an easy task. Many people fall at the first hurdle with the realisation that there is no quick solution, and that what they had dreamed of takes up far too much of their time to make it worthwhile or viable. But with focus and hard work, you can realise your dream, and this book will save you time in getting there.

The world is ready to hear us, and hear us, it must.

Part One: Becoming A Writer

There are some fundamental stages you need to work through to achieve your writing goals and publish your LGBTQ+ book. These include:

- Concept: What are you going to write about? What is your message going to be to the world?
- Planning: What is the purpose of your book? Who is the audience? What is your budget?
- Development: Establishing structure, fact and flow.
- First Draft: Getting it all down, not worrying about editing at this stage.
- Second Draft: You have finished and made your book as best it can be, with spelling and grammar checked.
- Editing: Handing it over to a professional editor.
- Proofreading: Check spellings, typos, grammar and paragraphing.
- Final Draft: All amendments made.
- Design: Formatting and cover design.
- Publication.
- Marketing.

All these very important steps are covered in Parts Two and Three. In Part One, we will look at what it takes to be a writer, and how to overcome any doubts you may have about the exciting and fulfilling journey you are about to embark on.

First, let me tell you a little about my own self-publishing journey and how I came to write this book.

1. Telling *their* Story: David Ledain

I have always been a writer. You will hear that many times from authors and writers. It is a cliché, but it is something that is innate and irresistible with in us.

I had dabbled in some form of writing since my early childhood, but it wasn't until I was in my late forties that I finally got round to writing my first, full-length novel.

Like many teenagers, especially those dealing with conflicts around sexuality, I spent hours crafting words of angst, in my case to the tunes of David Bowie, just trying to make sense of everything. I also kept diaries, which have proven a fascinating resource to look back on. By expressing myself this way, I was able to articulate how I felt about myself, though at the time I did not know it. I was effectively using writing as a form of therapy, trying to work out who I was and how I fitted into a straight world.

Writing as a job that I could earn money from, wasn't a life-choice that was open to me, or even something that crossed my mind. I scraped through secondary education with a couple of O levels in art and English. Later, I attended creative writing classes, but any ideas I had knocking around inside my head never got beyond an outline or the first couple of chapters. It was only many years later, that I finally sat down to write that full-blown novel many of us know we have inside us.

At that time, I was a stay-at-home dad, and my two sons were growing up fast and needed less of my time. With the advent of home computers, and the internet, I was able to work on a germ of an idea I'd had to create a story big enough to fill a novel. The internet provided me with a worldwide library of information and research on my topic that just wouldn't have been feasible a few years earlier.

My first novel took me four years to research and write. I approached agents with the manuscript, waiting interminably for the rejection letters, saying that they liked my work but that 'it wasn't quite the sort of book they had a position for at the moment'. I sent it out to prospective agents with a similar lack of joy before I discovered something called self-publishing, made easy via the internet.

The thought then occurred to me: why wait for rejection letters, when I knew that even if an agent did take me on there was no guarantee that a publishing house would? And even then, it might be years before the market was right for my book, once they'd changed the title, designed a cover, changed characters, and asked for any number of other amendments to be made, which of course, they would be perfectly entitled to do since they would be investing hugely to make me, and my book, a success. But I wasn't prepared to wait on the slim chance of that happening, so I researched everything I could find on self-publishing and spoke to those who had done it.

With anticipation of great things I self-published my novel through Amazon and naïvely expected it to fly off the virtual shelves, but to my surprise, even with the whole world hooked up online, my book did not sell many copies. I tried some marketing, approaching my local newspaper, which had a readership of twenty-nine thousand, and had an article about me and my book published in the paper. I thought at least that would generate a few sales. How wrong I was.

This was a sharp wake-up call to the world of self-publishing.

A friend of mine who had published a children's book through a small press, and had a very bad experience with them as they went bust, agreed that he too found it difficult to get his name out there, or to create any interest in his book. We wondered if there were other budding authors in our area who were facing the same problems, and how much more we could do if we combined the expertise and contacts of a few of these local independent authors. We set up a cooperative group called Chindi (an abbreviation of Chichester Independent Authors). In the beginning, we had six members, and immediately set about holding a small book fair to coincide with World Book Day. We sold our books, put on workshops, and held a Q&A session with the authors. It was very successful, and the group went from strength to strength, holding lots of events to support, market, and nurture other local independent authors and writers. We formed our group into a Community Interest Company (CIC), wrote a book about our collective experiences of self-publishing, held panel discussions and ran a writing competition with the local newspaper group.

By then my personal life had hit a critical point. I was coming to terms with separating from, and eventually divorcing, my wife. We had a good relationship, but my sexuality was the barrier neither of us could overcome. I thought I was literally the only person that this had ever happened to, being a gay man in a heterosexual marriage. The internet again proved to be invaluable, and I came across a group of gay men who, like me, had married, and had kids and were in various stages of divorce, and coming out.

I searched for books about gay dads that I could draw on for support, but found nothing that spoke to me. There were autobiographies written by sports stars and celebrities about their coming out stories, there were books for single-sex couples wanting to adopt, and others giving advice about how to bring up a child within a gay relationship, but nothing about men in *my* situation. So, I decided to write that book myself. I approached the men I had met through the online support group and asked if they would be willing to share their stories. *Gay Dad – ten true stories of divorced gay men with kids, living in the UK today*, was the result. I was overwhelmed by their generosity in sharing their experiences, and the heartfelt positivity that shone through in their telling of their stories. What the book showed was that in the end, after what in most cases had been many years, sometimes decades of distress and trauma, for them, their wives and their children, there was a way through.

I knew that my book was important for other men in this situation, but writing it also helped in my own coming out process.

Promoting and marketing *Gay Dad* I knew was going to prove a challenge because I wanted to protect my children. It wasn't their choosing, after all, that I wrote it. I decided to publish the book under a penname, *David Ledain*, a name I chose by combining my mother's maiden name and Bowie's first name. I also employed a PR agent to promote the book.

The calls to speak on various radio programmes across the country came in, and I spent a morning at BBC Sussex in Brighton linking up to presenters on shows to talk about my book and my experiences as a gay dad. Other radio slots, including BBC Radio 4's Woman's Hour, came along on the back of that as did invitations to give talks to LGBTQ+ groups. I was even contacted by an American TV station inviting me to appear in a documentary. Bloggers, reviewers, and internet magazines ran pieces about *Gay Dad*. It was such a different experience to the deafening silence that followed the launch of my novel.

Had I been 'visible' I could have accepted many more offers from major magazines and daily newspapers who wanted to run spreads, as well as do TV interviews, but I couldn't, and I had no qualms about that. My children were always my first consideration.

I had also finished writing a sequel to my first novel, which I launched at the same time as *Gay Dad* to gauge the difference in marketing and promotional opportunities each of these books generated. As with my first novel, I marketed the sequel myself. The difference between that and *Gay Dad* was stark, and it made me realise that the world was far more interested in me and my personal story than it was in my fiction writing.

Any dream I may have had to give up work and support myself through writing seemed very unlikely. For every sale of one of my novels it seemed I had to sweat blood, even with the help and support of my group of fellow indie authors. *Gay Dad*, on the other hand, sold by itself, steadily, with not much effort from me.

Was there another way? Would it even be possible to make a living writing non-fiction?

1.1 Fiction v Non-Fiction

As so few people were getting to see my novels, I set up a website, Twitter, and Facebook accounts to support and market them, but I found it increasingly difficult to keep uploading relevant content that would entice an audience. It seemed nothing I did made any difference to my sales online. The only sales of physical books of any significant number were those I made on stalls, or at speaking events with my fellow Chindi authors. Some might say that this was a reflection on the quality of my books and writing, but the truth is this is the plight of countless independent fiction writers. They are up against so many established and bestselling authors, with large publishing houses and huge marketing budgets behind them, with widespread access to all the high street outlets, it makes it almost impossible to compete with or even be a visible alternative.

On the other hand, my non-fiction book sold relatively well, and people were more than happy to talk to me about it. People were buying *Gay Dad* online because they were actively seeking out LGBTQ+ books on that topic; a book they identified with and that had meaning in their lives.

Fiction is a matter of taste, non-fiction, in all its myriad varieties, is life enhancing.

For newly emerging, independent writers, there is one message and truth that cannot be denied: to shift the number of copies to make debut fiction worthwhile, you need a hefty budget and an excessive amount of luck. If you are not constantly marketing your new novel, after the initial buzz in the first few weeks of its launch, sales will inevitably drop off, and eventually flatline. It is true to say that this happened with both my novels, but was not the case with my non-fiction book.

A question often asked is, is writing non-fiction more profitable than writing fiction? From what I have found, I believe it can be, and certainly for new, self-published authors. The eureka moment came for me when I realised this; that to make enough book sales to spend more time writing fiction, if that's what I wanted to do, I should be concentrating on promoting my non-fiction.

The nudges required to steer someone towards buying fiction are numerous and complex. It is said that to get someone to buy anything new, they need to have seen it seven times before they make the decision to buy. In fact, when there is so much choice, getting anyone to buy your book at all is an achievement in itself. Saying that, there has never been a better time to write and have your LGBTQ+ story read by a wide audience.

One of the big advantages is organic online discoverability which is aided by topical SEOs (search engine optimisation) where words relating to your topic and book can be picked up by search engines such as Google. Type 'Gay Dad book' in and my book comes up on the first listings page. This is hugely powerful as it means that anyone looking for such a book, not necessarily knowing the full title or author name, but just those few words, will be shown a list that includes my book. The importance of this cannot be understated as it is estimated that 95% of forward traffic is generated through first page listings, and 75% of users never scroll beyond that first page.

Achieving comparable search engine results for fiction is much more difficult because of the non-specific nature of fiction titles. Unless you know the title of the novel, or the name of the author you're interested in, you're much less likely to stumble across it via a random search.

Another thing worth noting is that non-fiction rightly occupies a higher price bracket, because what is being sold is knowledge, and that the author has spent a lot of time researching and collating that knowledge into a book people want to buy to improve themselves and enrich their lives.

If you've published a work of fiction, and have an author platform with a website and social media already, you might be wondering how easy it is to then publish in a completely different genre such as LGBTQ+ non-fiction without confusing your audience, or worse, turning them off altogether. Does having a duo, or multi-genre book portfolio prove disadvantageous? I chose to keep my non-fiction entirely separate by writing under a penname and I set-up a website and social media platforms to match. The opinion in the traditional publishing world is that authors should stick to, and ideally specialise in, just one genre because agents and publishers cannot afford to reinvent a writer's brand with every new book. The self-published author doesn't have those same constraints, but if you are moving from fiction to non-fiction, you will still need to think about how you're going to do that. Some authors invent new pennames and brands for each sub-genre they write in. This is absolutely fine, but you are then very dependent on the strength and popularity of each individual book to carry it forward.

One of the central tenets of self-publishing, is that you are free to choose what you want to write about, and not be pigeonholed.

After the relative success of *Gay Dad*, I decided to step back from the group and fiction writing and to concentrate on LGBTQ+ non-fiction. I wrote a book called *This Forbidden Fruit – Male Homosexuality: A Culture and History Guide.*

This book came about as a result of my research for *Gay Dad,* when I realised how much gay culture and history I didn't know. I couldn't understand why that should be. I'd been around a fair while yet there was such a lot of LGBTQ+ information that simply wasn't readily available or easily accessible, which had passed me by. It wasn't taught in schools and certainly wasn't something talked about in the public domain and yet the involvement of gay men and women in the arts, in popular culture, in serving their country in all sorts of extraordinary ways has been incredible. Simply put, without the minds and skills of LGBTQ+ people throughout history, the world would be a very different and less artistically stimulating place.

At about this time, producer and scriptwriter, Nicholas McInerny, who came across *Gay Dad*, asked me to join a discussion panel with other gay and bi dads on a series of podcasts called *Rainbow Dads*. It was nominated for the Podcast Awards in 2019.

My third non-fiction book, *Having Gay Sex – A Guide to Male Homosexual Sex*, again came about because of the lack of knowledge and misconceptions about what men get up to when they have sex together. It is still a mystery that holds a fascination for many and stops many more men from realising their true selves.

All my books are aimed at filling gaps. They are books that I could not find elsewhere and so decided to write myself. That is the fundamental objective; to identify the book you want to write and to produce it.

1.2 Using A Penname

Whatever the subject matter, it cannot be a book written by anyone other than you.

But how much of yourself do you want to expose to the public?

Think about this carefully. The 'public' is not a nebulous group that is silent somewhere beyond your reach. It is important to understand that their reactions to what you do and say can affect you or your life. 'Public' means those people living in your town, city or living next door, even your own family members (aunties, uncles, cousins), who may not know the fantastic, heartrending story you are about to launch on to an unsuspecting world. In your book you might talk about your coming out story, about sexual matters, about all sorts of things that might shock some people. It could be that your story appears in the local paper, on social media, or even be picked up by the national press and radio. Do you really want everybody, including work colleagues and friends to read a detailed, intimate, true life-story and make that connection between you, your book and your family?

The first thing to consider is that it might be better to change all the names of everyone involved in your story. While some, like Aunty Dot, will be perfectly happy for you to tell your story, her children might not like to be so closely associated and easily recognisable. As well as changing their names, all other references to those close to you should be disguised enough so they cannot be identified unless you have had their full agreement to do so. Even then, you should make it clear to them that some people might regard your book in a negative way and use it to slander anyone who has a connection to it. Protecting loved ones must always be at the forefront of your mind.

Think hard about whether you want to use your real name or a penname.

The penname I chose resonates with a certain air of theatricality, but more importantly it is distinctive and memorable (although sometimes people pronounce it incorrectly). I continue to use that penname rather than my birth name, one, because I believe it still gives some barrier of protection to my family, and also because it has grown into a successful brand. It also gives me the power to talk freely about gay topics without a filter, which writing under my given name and thinking about my family, I might subconsciously slip into. To revert to my real name, or to change to a new penname, would be confusing to my audience and time-consuming for me to build up new lists of followers on social media. Even when I explain this to people there is still sometimes an air of suspicion or confusion as if I am trying to hide something.

LGBTQ+ people have always been obliged to 'explain' themselves, this is nothing new.

Cameron D. James is a prolific author of gay erotica and writes under several different pennames. He only recently put aside a couple of podcasts he hosted which specifically targeted different sections of his readers. I asked him how he managed to juggle all these pennames in the busy world of social media. Does he have a vast wall-mounted spreadsheet with all the relevant information for each genre and the allocated pennames he writes under? And if one book is not selling, does he make a swift and calculated decision to ditch it?

'The biggest thing I've had to learn is that I take on too much and I have to step back sometimes. I no longer do the podcasts for that reason. The multiple pennames are all very different, so it's not hard for me to keep them apart. So, Cameron D. James is the name for my generic gay romance books and Dylan James is the penname for my gay young adult books. But I have other names for different genres in taboo and very kinky gay stuff, and yet another for straight stories. When I'm on social media I simply have to get into the mindset of those different genres.

I create new pennames, because, as I write, I realise something doesn't fit with the penname I have, so I create a new one to fit that story.

I do keep a spreadsheet of sales stats and I know that certain taboo subjects sell well, and gay young adult fiction is by far my bestselling genre. I try to publish at least one book a year under each penname, but it is all revenue driven.'

Once people know that you use a penname, the first thing they ask is how you came about it. Choosing a name for your new writing ego is great fun, but take your time and consider it carefully. Think about the image you want to project. What does the name conjure in your mind? Could there be any other connotation, perhaps one that is not so flattering?

Consider also how easy it is to pronounce and spell. Although having a name that people have to ask whether they are saying it or spelling it correctly does have added memorable sticking value, but making it sound clear and instantly recognisable should be the aim. Does the first name sound right with the surname? Can you imagine that name on the cover of your book, and in your chosen genre? Google the name to make sure there is no one else of note with the same.

Hearing someone say your newly invented name for the first time feels odd. It's as if there is a stranger standing behind you, but you soon acquire it as your own, and quickly learn to recognise it and answer to it. It can get a bit confusing if you're talking to a group of people where some know you by your penname, and others by your given name.

Writers use pennames for many reasons. Female writers, writing predominantly for a male audience will sometimes choose to use their initials and surname to counter any preconceived ideas by potential readers. In the nineteenth century it was very difficult for women to get published at all. The Brontë sisters, for instance, first approached their publishers pretending to be three gentlemen brothers. Thankfully, these days there are less overt prejudices, but still writers of any gender might choose a penname for many different reasons.

It is unlikely that a penname by itself will make the difference between your book being a success or not.

It may help to get it noticed, and keep you, the author, secret from family members or work colleagues; and having different pennames for different genres of writing can stop confusion when readers cross from one to another, but the biggest plus to acquiring a penname is the protection it affords others.

2. Publishers And Agents

Another plus to writing non-fiction is that most traditional publishers, if you are thinking of going that route, or indeed, University presses if your book is academically focused, don't require it to be submitted through an agent. Instead, what they ask for is a proposal which allows the author to pitch their idea without having to commit to a year or more of research and writing before a commission on the book is agreed. However, proposals are not a brief synopsis, so you will have to do a lot of preliminary work. But there is nothing to say that you cannot have your book editor-ready at the time of submitting a proposal.

A full proposal will be anything between fifteen and fifty pages long. It should be the blueprint of your book together with a financial plan of how it is going to make money. It should include the following:

- Title page with author name and credentials, such as PhD, Dr., MBE, CEO, or a relevant title you might be introduced as on a panel. For instance, gay dad, bisexual Sikh, or a trans woman healthcare leader. This page should also include a strapline. Use your back-of-book blurb as a guide.
- The proposal table of contents.
- Overview of your book, including word count and page number if you know them, but certainly the length you project your book to be. The unique premise and why are you the most qualified person to write it. The LGBTQ+ tag alone will not be enough. What are you, the author, setting out to prove, examine, share, or explore? What is the motive behind your book and the reasons for writing it?

- About the author. Your backstory, your struggles and how and why you came up with the idea for this book. Include any previous books you've published, articles you've had printed, podcasts and panels you've appeared on, etc.
- Competition – other books on the market that are close to your proposed idea and why yours will be unique. Don't hide the fact that there are other books out there, but your book cannot be so similar that it is difficult to differentiate it. Try to find half a dozen titles and research them. A market without any books on your subject might just indicate that it is so niche that there simply isn't a big enough demand for it. However, your market might be very small and that is still valid if you can show that it is made up of book buyers who have an interest in your subject. The LGBTQ+ market is very supportive, but you want to try to show that your book can reach beyond that community alone.
- Marketing – how are you going to market your book. How will you convey your message via social media and other media? Think of your primary customer and then other groups of people who might have an interest in the subject.
- The book table of contents.
- Chapter by chapter outline/synopsis.
- One or two sample chapters.

All of the above bullet points are worth considering for anyone about to write their book.

For more in-depth detail on how to write a proposal, go to blog.reedsy.com.

You could also look to smaller, independent publishers. HarperCollins, Penguin, MacMillan, and such have huge power and influence, but smaller, indie publishers often hold what they call 'un-agented' submission windows for authors who do not have an agent. Check out the *Writers' and Artists' Yearbook* for agents and publishers. It is a mine of book industry related information, including articles written by LGBTQ+ writers, as well as a list of LGBTQ+ publishers under the heading *Publishers of Fiction and Publishers of Non-Fiction Indexes*. The internet group *Out On The Page* also provide a valuable LGBTQ+ resource to subscribers, with lists of agents, small presses, courses, workshops, events, festivals and much more. Also, Penguin run the WriteNow programme which aims to, 'find, nurture and publish new writers from communities under-represented on the nation's book-shelves', and self-published authors are eligible to apply.

Publishers of all sizes receive huge numbers of manuscripts and each month try to process what is called the slush-pile; the unsolicited query letters and manuscripts sent in by authors. They simply don't have the time, or the number of people required to read through fifty to a hundred manuscripts each week, as well as work with those authors they do have contracts with. Always read the submission guidelines available on all agents' and publisher' websites before you send anything in.

Unfortunately, writing for minority, niche audiences, such as the LGBTQ+ community, is not the scale big publishing houses work to. They are essentially only interested in volume of sales, and anything not within the narrow constrains of 'the norm', unless its earth-shattering, is not worth their time and money investing in. Most publishing houses do have authors from diverse LGBTQ+ backgrounds on their catalogues, which ironically means they have less need for anymore. Add to this the small number of LGBTQ+ specific publishers, a consequence of mainstream equality, and it is clear how difficult it is for LGBTQ+ writers to get recognition.

Make sure you have thoroughly researched your target publishers beforehand, and don't let a desire to be traditionally published get you hooked into something suspect which could end up costing you hundreds, possibly thousands of pounds, and for nothing.

An agent will help to negotiate a contract with a prospective publisher and what can be achieved financially, as well as have a good understanding of the business and what is saleable to the industry. That is their job. As with any business relationship, check your agent's credentials, what they say they are going to offer you and what they will take as their cut, very carefully before signing with them. If you want an agent, you need to find a good one you can trust who will move things forward for you, but it will still take time to get the interest of a publisher.

The traditional publishing route is notoriously slow. Publishers will frequently stipulate that you submit your manuscript only to them rather than mailing it out to every publisher you can find at the same time. Even when you have a signed contract, like most bestselling authors, you will find you are constantly writing to deadlines, and yet a finished book is often at the publishers' months, possibly up to two years before it is scheduled to be launched and hits the shelves.

2.1 Partnership Publishing

It is not just the research and creativity of writing that I enjoy, but also working closely with cover designers, editors, and other professionals, that gives me the impetus to do what I love doing – creating a book from start to finish. I would be doing you an injustice, however, to say that your full involvement in every aspect of the process was essential and that this is the only way it can be done. For some, the idea of managing so many spinning plates at once when all they really want to do is write, is terrifying. So much so that it can spell the end of a much-loved manuscript that would otherwise be telling the world a uniquely fascinating LGBTQ+ story. There is another way.

For a not insubstantial fee, partnership publishing companies will support authors and typically handle the publishing process for them from editing to formatting and cover design, through to marketing, distribution, and promotion. They have cleverly filled a gap in the market between self-publishing and what used to be called 'vanity publishing'. Vanity publishing basically meant uploading anything that vaguely resembled a typed manuscript, having it made into a book and printing off as many copies as was required for a set price. A process not dissimilar to the way in which you might upload photographs to a website to have them made into a photo album you can share with your family.

Partnership publishers have refined that process. They are able to pay higher royalties than traditional publishers; lower, however, than self-published authors can earn doing it all for themselves. There is also no guarantee that by entering into a contract with a partnership publisher that it will reap more sales, though with a distribution element in the deal, you might calculate that this is worth it. Some will require you to submit your manuscript for assessment before they agree to work with you.

Again, if this is something that appeals to you, do research what other companies offer before you sign anything. Look at other authors' reviews of the company. Do they have books like yours in their catalogue? Are any of their authors LGBTQ+? Find and talk to other authors who have used them. What has their experience been like? Above all, know the costs involved, and stick to your budget. Some companies will offer each element of the publishing process separately, meaning you can cherry-pick exactly what you want. Others will offer to do it all from beginning to end, but whichever you choose, you need to factor-in that you might never recoup the costs.

One author I spoke to, an historical fiction writer, used The Book Guild, part of the Troubador Publishing Group. 'As for sales, and based on royalties I've made over the first six month period,' she said, 'at the same level it will take me about five years to recoup my publication costs with them, and this doesn't include what I'd already paid out for editing and having a professional cover designed. I also didn't receive the amount of help I expected from them when it came to marketing, but perhaps that was me being a bit over-optimistic.'

She went on to say, 'if you have the money, and don't want the hassle of formatting, for instance, it can be worth it. I received a generous allocation of free books, and with a publisher like this you do have the benefit of their distribution network. Just don't expect to sit back and let them do all the work of promotion for you though. This applies to all publishers, even the biggest and most mainstream. They spend little money on marketing and promotion. I've decided that I will self-publish my next book. If I must sell it myself, I might as well take control of the whole process and save the money as well.'

My advice concerning partnership publishing is to really think about what you want from the whole writing and publishing experience. Do you want to have total control, or are you happy to let responsibility for certain aspects be taken over at a cost? If this direction is the way you want to go, you absolutely must research the company you are intending to use thoroughly, including all the contract small print before you commit.

2.2 Book Distribution

One thing that traditional publishing offers, which is hard to replicate in self-publishing, is the distribution network. Major high street bookshops and supermarket book buyers, as well as independent bookshop owners, get their stock from wholesalers, the middlemen who buy books in bulk direct from the publishers at a discounted price, which is usually about 55% off the retail price, before then selling on to the retailers. Wholesale companies produce regularly updated catalogues, of their available stock, either every month, or every quarter, by book title, author name, publisher and ISBN (International Standard Book Number).

Some wholesalers are not averse to stocking books by small publishers but only if they can guarantee delivery to their warehouse whenever they place an order. These people are in the business of making money, and they are only interested in books that will sell in the thousands. Competition for the purchasing power of major book selling outlets is understandably fierce, and if a book is not published with advance notice, if it's by an unknown author or publisher, and not listed with the main wholesalers, it's unlikely to be considered by any of the major retailers. Self-publishing your book without a publishing company of some reputable size behind you, virtually excludes you from getting into the major distributor's catalogues.

What about independent bookshops because they are at least somewhere you'd think self-published authors would be welcomed to have their books stocked and sold? Well, maybe.

Independent bookshop owners will have preferences of which distributors they use, because of things such as ease of delivery, exclusivity discounting, or simply that they like the people they deal with over the phone. Therefore, getting even independent book sellers to notice your book and want to stock it is a challenge.

Unlike well-known high street shops that have plenty of backroom storage and a higher turnover of stock, independent bookshops have far less space. They cannot afford to have books on their shelves that do not sell. When considering whether to take your book or not they will want to see some proof beyond the physical quality of the book that you are serious about wanting to help them sell it. They will look for good four and five-star reviews on Amazon and Goodreads, that you have a reasonable following on social media, and ideally that you have a strong voice in your LGBTQ+ community. If people know your name, bookshop owners are more likely to stock your book.

At the time of writing there are very few LGBTQ+ specific bookshops in the UK: *Gay's The Word* in London, *Category Is* in Glasgow, *The Portal Bookshop* in York, and *Queer Lit*, an online bookstore which also has a bricks and mortar shop in Manchester. Most bookshops stock LGBTQ+ books and may even have a gender and sexuality section or shelf, and it appears that independent bookshops have been making a comeback despite the downturn of overall trade in traditional town centres.

The high street is changing and will continue to do so, but renewed interest in independent bookshops means that they can offer an essential hub for the community, much in the same way that independent local pubs do. Large book chains have adopted the café culture of the 1990s and 2000s, by creating a relaxed ambience in which to sit and read with a coffee, but what they lack is the sense of community. Independent bookshops often have all sorts of other activities going on in-store other than selling books based on the needs of their immediate area and the diverse communities living there. They are usually open to suggestions and often hold author evenings, readings, or talks. You just need to approach them with your idea, but make sure that it is financially beneficial to both parties.

If you can build relationships with the owners of independent bookshops in your town or city, especially those that are LGBTQ+ allies, and ensure that you can regularly supply them with your book at a reasonable discount (usually between 35–40% off the cover price), you will find you can create your own small distribution network by keeping a stock yourself. 'Author copies' can be ordered at a reduced print cost from your online publisher and means you can keep as many or as few as you need.

2.3 Amazon

Putting aside any ethical issues that surround Amazon, let us talk for a moment about the grip Amazon Books has on the market. Is it really the world's largest bookstore? Amazon lists some 33 million titles for sale, and it is estimated that a new book is added to its virtual shelves every few minutes. It is the largest retailer of e-books. Its main competitors are Apple iBooks, Nook, Kobo, and Google Play.

According to Patrick Snow, an international bestselling author and publishing coach, and said with a certain amount of tongue-in-cheek irony, 'If you want to be a bestselling author, take out a $100,000 loan and buy 15,000 copies of your own book from Amazon'.

Amazon remain tight-lipped about how their ranking algorithms work. They do provide sales stats, but not information about what exactly it takes to rise up the rankings to become a bestseller. Numbers bandied about by those who have researched this say that, typically, there needs to be fast and furious initial purchasing of your book to get it anywhere near the radar of Amazon's 'Bestseller Top 100' lists.

The suggested minimum number of sales to hit bestseller lists, is between 500 and 1,000 copies sold across all platforms and, since the industry thinking is that Amazon accounts for 30% of print sales, a title hitting the top five will have to sell approximately 300 print copies each day through Amazon, depending on the day of the week and time of the year. Note, rankings change all the time, so a continuous upward trajectory is essential to stay in the ranking lists. It is also worth noting that other top 100 bestseller lists, such as that of the New York Times, require sales in the first week of publication to hit 9000 copies. To reach such giddying heights takes a lot of marketing, money, and knowhow. Throwing $100,000 dollars on its own at a book still won't necessarily create enough interest to sustain a meaningful position in the rankings for very long.

E-books can reach the top of niche categories fairly easily, with give-aways and countdown deals, but these rankings change very quickly. Keep a close eye on them and use high ranking top three positions to your advantage by sharing screen shots on social media.

What Amazon does do so proficiently is to offer readers the opportunity of finding something they didn't know they wanted, and that's where the tags you apply when setting up your book on any digital platform can help people interested in your LGBTQ+ specific topic to find it. If your book sells, it will also appear in the 'Also Bought' banner, showing other readers similar books to those they are interested in.

Getting reviews, especially good five-star reviews, will also get your book spotted by the Amazon algorithms.

There are sites online where you can purchase promotional advertising to help boost your book's profile but be careful not to exceed your budget and be aware also that these ads will not, in themselves, increase sales.

The simplicity of using the internet to shop attracts a lot of people, but it can also be the anonymity of it that draws people to shop online. It might be easier and safer, for instance, for someone to download a LGBTQ+ e-book straight to their Kindle, than have a parcel arrive at home where other members of the family or household might intercept it.

There are disadvantages to Amazon. Not every e-book reader uses a Kindle and not every book customer uses Amazon. There are other e-book platforms, such as Kobo and Nook, and many people still love the tactile nature and ambience of browsing in a bricks and mortar bookshop.

If you are considering multi-platform publication you will need to look into the benefits and disadvantages of doing so as this will affect the percentage value of your royalty pay-outs.

Amazon offer other benefits for 90 days exclusivity through KDP Select, which you can sign up to when you publish, such as visibility on the Kindle Store and automatic addition to KU (Kindle Unlimited), a subscription service where royalties are paid by the number of pages read rather than books sold.

After one month of your publication date on Amazon you can run a 99p countdown deal on your e-book. These run for one week, and you can do this once in any three-month period. If doing a countdown deal, contact anyone you sent a complimentary copy of your book to and ask them to purchase the 99p e-book version as well so that they can leave a verified purchaser review on Amazon. Explain how important reviews are, that you really appreciate their support, and send them the link to the review page.

Although Amazon has a huge proportion of the market, what's left is still worth going for, and while relying on Amazon in the short to medium term as you build your audience might not be a bad thing, once you start to make serious revenue, it might be better to spread your assets. If, for instance, Amazon suddenly decided to change an algorithm or to reduce their royalty levels, you could see your income reduce significantly overnight.

For the first-time, independent author, this can all seem like a minefield, knowing what to do for the best, but keeping things as straightforward as possible is probably the best advice when you've got so much else going on with your marketing and promotion.

2.4 IngramSpark

If you are feeling confident and you have the time, and crucially your budget will allow for it, publishing your book through IngramSpark has the benefit of getting it listed on their online database, through which any bookshop or library can order single copies or larger quantities. That still won't mean that you will start to see your book on the shelves at your local supermarket, Waterstones, or W.H. Smiths, but it will give you increased distribution, and there is nothing to stop you then from working with your local high street stores to encourage them to stock your book. Publishing with IngramSpark will also mean that your e-book will be available to readers who use Kobo or Nook.

Having your book with IngramSpark does not mean you cannot also publish through KDP (Kindle Direct Publishing, Amazon's online publishing service), and the best advice is to do both. You will however need to purchase your own ISBN from Nielson, currently £89 for one or £164 for ten (check their up to date prices). Use the same ISBN for both IngramSpark and KDP. If you use different ISBNs your book could end up with duplicate entries on Amazon and that will cause issues, which could mean both entries being taken down until it is resolved.

You will also need to create your own 'publishing company' name that will link to your ISBN, because distributors like IngramSpark, list every book in their catalogue by author, title, ISBN and publisher. This doesn't mean you have to declare yourself to HMRC, but it might be advisable to seek expert accounting advice if your royalty revenue starts to build beyond the current trading allowance laws in the UK, which enables anyone to earn £1,000 from a hobby before they need to pay tax (check Gov.org for latest tax details).

When thinking about a publishing name, think what might attract attention and sound like a legitimate publishing company that would have you and your book in its catalogue. Your name by itself as the publisher might not be enough for a small independent bookshop owner to invest in. Think of the overall LGBTQ+ community you are appealing to. If you are planning on future books, you don't then want to have to consider a new publisher name because this one doesn't fit.

IngramSpark charge a set-up fee to upload your book and e-book (check current prices), whereas KDP is free, but the advantages of the distribution IngramSpark can bring could make that investment worthwhile.

If using both KDP and IngramSpark, do not click the 'Expanded Distribution' button when setting up on KDP. For one thing your royalty level will be lower, but also expanded distribution will allow your book to be listed on the IngramSpark catalogue but with Amazon as the publisher and this might put off independent bookshops.

Setting the discount level to standard on IngramSpark will mean that they will get 15% and the bookshop gets 40%, plus unsold books are returnable which is a good incentive for small businesses. You can also use IngramSpark for hardcover copies if you want a special run of your book for promotions.

3. Telling *their* Story: Gary H. James

Gary H. James first started writing his coming out story years before publishing his book *Beyond the Closet*. Here, he tells me why it took him so long and what stopped him from doing it sooner.

I first started writing my book *Beyond the Closet* over fifteen years ago when I was not that long into my new life as a gay man. I was scared and stubborn and didn't want to be seen as a stereotypical gay man. I was struggling with telling friends and family, and I wanted the world to know just how difficult it was for a gay man to come out.

I didn't want to come out. I was fearful of rejection and scorn, especially from the people I loved. It all felt very unfair to me. I hadn't chosen to be attracted to the same sex and I still felt like the same person I was when I had a girlfriend. But it felt like other people's impressions of me would change.

I decided to write a book based on my own experiences of coming out to explain the process to those who will never have to go through it. My hope is to educate, particularly, straight people, to what it is like and what life as a gay man at the start of the new millennium was all about.

What I didn't realise at the time was that writing my book was actually a cathartic journey. It helped me to come to terms with my sexuality and be happy in my own skin.

I returned to the book many times over the past fifteen years, but I always seemed to hit a wall. It was mostly the fear of having to come out again and deal with the unknown responses. I don't think I had come to terms with it myself and I needed more time. Also, I had convinced myself that a book about me essentially moaning, wasn't going to be of interest to anyone else.

Suddenly, last year, I felt a fire in my belly. I needed to finish my book; I needed people to read my story because it felt to me that it represented a lot of other gay people's stories too. I opened my laptop and began to write and edit again. I got some great advice from a couple of friends who read through the first draft versions and they gave me the extra confidence I needed to continue with it. They were able to give objective criticism that I was too close to my book to do myself. This year with all the craziness that has gone on with the Coronavirus, I had the extra time I needed to complete the book. I pushed through the pain barrier and am ecstatic to finally have my book out for people to read. Am I still a bit scared? Of course, but I know in my heart that I've done the right thing.

It's the starting point for me and I'm excited to see how readers will rate and review my book. Regardless though, I am so proud to be able to say that I have written and published my own book.

My story begins at the end of 1999 – already, in just twenty short years, gay rights and society have moved on so much. I am the second youngest in a family of four children. My father was in the army and we travelled between the UK and Germany every few years with his work. It was a very macho environment and with two older brothers, I was surrounded by testosterone. That said, it was probably obvious to everyone in my family that I wasn't a very boyish boy. I was never really into sports and I loved dancing and singing and dressing up.

In my teenage years I was definitely horny and had several girlfriends, but I was always a gentleman and tended to go out with girls rather than just kiss and tell. When I was sixteen, I fell for a girl at school and we stayed together for seven years.

It was not long after we split up that an innocent question on a night out with work mates led to me questioning my sexuality. I had never been brave enough to acknowledge certain feelings I'd had until this point. Suddenly I had the chance to put them to the test. An encounter with a work colleague, sent me looking back through my life, looking for clues to help me work out if I was gay or not. I was surprised at just how many things my mind had blocked out.

Once it became obvious to me that I was gay, it was time to navigate the stormy waters of coming out to those nearest and dearest to me, as well as complete strangers. I had to learn what it was like being a gay man in the noughties. At the age of twenty-three my life had irreversibly changed, and I now had to figure out what that meant to me and those around me. I was excited but also petrified and all the gay shame that I had been brought up with, resurfaced. I didn't know if I had the balls to go through with it, but I couldn't live a lie either.

Beyond the Closet concentrates on a period of approximately ten years of my life and how I dealt with coming out. It tells how I fell in love, faced my fears and managed to avoid police intervention when coming out to one particular family member!

Today, I live in the suburbs of London with my husband and although I do have some friends who are gay, the majority of my friends are straight. For some, the gay scene is part of being gay and for others they feel the scene represents a stereotype. I have learned that neither of those views is wrong. It is completely down to the individual. But the more representation gay people have in society in all their guises, the more the stereotype of what a gay man is, or should be, will evolve.

I have been really fortunate in the acceptance I've received from friends and family, but perhaps my harshest critic has always been me. Reading my book back now, I feel gay rights and acceptance have come on leaps and bounds since I came out. I am ashamed by some of the feelings and fears I've relived in my book, but I needed to be completely honest about that time in my life. Society was different twenty years ago and different again in the twenty years prior to that, when I was growing up.

I think I've made positive steps forward in my personal battle with being gay in that time. I still believe that who I love or am attracted to shouldn't define me or who I choose to be friends with. It is a journey that we're all on and I'm pleased to say that I'm more comfortable than ever with being gay.

As a non-scene gay, I also wanted to give a different take on the coming out genre. I wanted to tell a tale of an ordinary boy who thought he would grow up, get married and start a family. Just because I turned out to be attracted to the same sex, I didn't feel like my desire to be monogamous and settle down needed to change. Children are a different matter and despite there being several ways for two men to start a family, it's something that I've decided I don't want strongly enough.

Releasing this book has been another big step. I am coming out yet again and I don't think I will ever truly stop coming out. There will always be a situation where it's unclear about the relationship between me and my husband, or it might be a simple assumption that people wonder where my wife is, for instance. The truth is it does get easier and with society moving on too, that will only continue to improve.

Everyone has their own story and I hope that by sharing mine someone out there might feel less alone. Coming out binds all gay people. Be proud of yourself – there is only one of you!

Gary H. James' book *Beyond the Closet* is available on Amazon. Gary can be found on Twitter @GJ_EntFocus

4. Building Blocks

We all suffer with self-doubt every now and then, so let's look at some fundamental things that will aid, strengthen, and embolden you in writing your LGBTQ+ book.

4.1 Time

When it comes to forging a 'career' as a writer, there is a consensus of timescale for how long it takes an unestablished writer to become a fully-fledged, self-supporting, author. With the wind in the right direction and a good deal of luck, it could take as long as ten years to reach a position that enables giving up the day job. Some will gain self-sustainability within three to five years, or maybe sooner, but whatever the actual length of time, success does not come overnight, or without a tremendous amount of work and tenacity. Your personal success goals might also be very different to someone else's.

There will always be individual stories of apparent instant success for us to admire, but it is well documented, and worth noting, that many mainstream popular authors spent years having their manuscripts rejected before they found an agent and publisher willing to take them on. Many writers actually start their writing careers in publishing, journalism, or editing, giving them an insight and the access to people they otherwise wouldn't have. There is also a huge amount of serendipity at play as well, and no successful writer got into writing as a way of making a quick buck. All their journeys to success are long and passionate and arduous.

People who want to write, but do not have the willpower or confidence to do so, often ask: how do I find the time?

The answer is simple. Essentially, you just do. For me, writing is not a chore but a pleasure, and when I have an end goal of completing a book, I write as-and-when I have the time, picking it up, and putting it down, but, importantly, keeping at it to some degree every day until I have completed the task. My first novel took me four years to finish.

Working to pay the bills, running a house, and bringing up children are all incredibly difficult to do while also finding the time to write. Some writers take time out of the family situation, taking themselves off on writing retreats, or hunkering down for a few days in a hotel to get away from the interruptions and distractions of home life, especially if they are at the final editing stages. Most writers will make the best of the time available to them, be it an hour here or a few hours there, to knock out a paragraph they've been thinking about, or do some editing. This they do between their daily tasks and responsibilities.

Honestly, and certainly if you are embarking on your first book, from the first word on the page to self-publishing and selling a few copies, it will take up to two years to accomplish. This is assuming you also work for a living and have other responsibilities outside of writing. Clearly if you are at home all day on your own, you will have more time.

When starting out, bear this in mind: don't expect to rattle off anything of substance in a few weeks or months. Do not put yourself under that sort of pressure. And anyone who tries to sell you the myth that you can achieve instant success in writing and publishing a book in super-quick time, with little effort, is marketing a falsehood entirely for their own profit, usually to get you to buy their own 'revolutionary' book and/or courses. The reality of it is, fast-tracking, and doing it without any involvement of skill or professional help along the way, will not give you what you dream of in the end result. You will end up wasting both your time and money.

I am sure that you will not be put off by the long, often solitary, road that lies ahead. You will continue to tap away at the keyboard no matter what. It is far better, instead of paying someone to give you an instant solution that will probably not be fulfilled, to simply get on and do it for yourself.

4.1.1 Planning the Road Ahead

It is, of course, always counter-productive to compare ourselves to others, but we all do it. What we should concentrate on, however, is where we currently are compared to where we were a year ago, and where we strive to be in two, three, or five years' time. A ten-year plan will rarely be stuck to, but at least having it sets out the milestones of where you want to be, allowing of course for things to change along the way, not least of which is everyday life.

Don't beat yourself up if you need to take time out; a week, a month, a year or two off-track could be what you need to sort out your work or family life, and to revitalise your energy and creativity when it is the right time to get back into writing again.

It is not a race, but hopefully you can adjust your work/life balance in such a way that it accommodates your writing. Remember, no one is going to criticise you over the late publication of your book, there are no agents or publishers hassling you, or breathing down your neck to meet deadlines. Your pace is entirely your decision. However, a schedule of where you want to be with your manuscript, edits, proofreading, etc. is not a bad thing, even if that gets rejigged several times when other things inevitably take priority. Give yourself a goal or a series of incrementally more challenging goals to aim for, and that will help motivate you to keep moving forward.

Make your timescale for achieving those goals something that you might actually meet. Rather than rushing to get your book written in time for the Christmas market, for instance, you might instead think ahead to next Christmas and take the pressure off yourself.

Here's a few tips on how to establish realistic deadlines and routines:

- Set short, medium, and long term deadlines for yourself. A short deadline might be to get some research done, or an email list together of people you need to interview. A medium length deadline might be to finish the book structure, sketching out the chapters, and section headings. A longer length deadline would be, the first draft, the first edits back from the editor, or the final manuscript.
- Break the writing you need to do down into manageable parts you can work on. Don't attempt to write the whole of your book in one smooth, linear exercise, starting at page one, and finishing at *The End* on page 250. Have a strategy for the number of chapters and sub-headings, and roughly plan the order you want to work on them. This need not be the actual order they will appear in your finished book, but might be based on ease of writing, smallest amount of research needed, the one you have most knowledge of, a trip to a certain location, or an interview you've got lined up. You will undoubtedly have the bones of at least one chapter – the LGBTQ+ idea around which you were inspired to write your book in the first place. This

might be chapter one, but it might equally be chapter 21. At this stage it isn't vital to know where that chapter will finally sit within your book, the important thing is to get started, and to build the other chapters around it.

- Set yourself honest and achievable routines. If you know you won't be able to write every day of the week, think in terms of how many days per week are reasonable and manageable for you. You might say that you can definitely do three days, but you might not be able to stick to the same three days every week. A routine is good, but many people find, despite all good intentions, that such routines just don't work for them. Be realistic. If you know you'll never stick to a rigid plan, make it looser. Just tell yourself 'I've got to get this chapter finished by the end of the week', or 'Before I sit down for something to eat tonight, I'll go over that section I wrote yesterday'. Some people thrive on achieving daily wordcounts, others find that too pressurising. Work with what works for you.
- Writing is a lonely routine and it's important to give yourself timeout. Putting your feet up for half an hour when you've finished writing for the day, or going for a long walk to clear your head can be just what you need.
- Knowing the best time of day for you to write is also very important. Some writers are literally up with the birds and thrashing it out on the keyboard before the rest of us have even stirred. Others perform better later in the day, or into the evening.
- Acknowledge your limits of concentration. A couple of hours might be plenty for you before you start to flag. When getting even one more word out starts to get painful, then is the time to stop, go off, and do something else.

4.2 Invest In Your Education

There are several options to creating the author life/career you want, these are:

1. Do nothing, and leave it all to chance by uploading your book onto Amazon. This will require a lot of faith and crossing of fingers if you are going to sell your book beyond your immediate family and friends.
2. Send your manuscript to agents and publishers and wait, and wait, and wait, and wait …
3. Do it slowly, incurring as little cost in both time and money as feasibly possible. This is not a bad option, but with small incremental steps, and without significant book sales, you are looking at years of selling your book on a non-profit basis. But there is nothing wrong with that.
4. Learn from others. Take a writing course, read about other people's experiences. Invest some time and a bit of money in educating yourself about marketing and how to promote your book.

By purchasing this book and taking the time to read it, you are actioning that last point. You are self-educating. You are investing a bit of time and money to broaden your understanding and knowledge of self-publishing. Afterall, how can we progress in anything, if we do not seek out the expertise and experience of those who have been on that same journey before us? We can't; we have to take that first step and seek out some knowledge.

Other writers provide a fount of untapped information and experience. If there is a writers' group near where you live, my advice would be to join it. Firstly, it will get your name out into the local community, but secondly, and more importantly, you will learn a lot about marketing and promotion first-hand from people who can give you all sorts of tips: how to contact local media, how to set up a stall at the local market, who you can connect, and collaborate with. If you can find an LGBTQ+ group, even better, because they will support you with any concerns you have about coming out so publicly or talking about your life, in your book.

There is no harm in investing in creative writing courses too, and quality instruction on how to improve your writing can only be a good thing. Doing this does not imply that you cannot write, but that you wish to hone your skills, and use the same grammatical techniques as any bestselling author.

Don't look at wanting to learn as a negative.

Read books on creative writing, and research online. There are plenty of non-fiction writing courses available and, dependant on your budget, you can find anything from a couple of hours tutorial run by a writing group, often at your local library, to a university degree course, and many others in between.

4.3 Find Fellow Authors

Follow as many LGBTQ+ writers on your social media as you can find, and anyone who has a particular interest in your subject. The online LGBTQ+ writers support network, Out On The Page, has a directory of LGBTQ+ writers and authors of all genres, as does QueerIndie.com.

Check the noticeboard in your local library for local writing groups or ask your friendly independent bookshop owner if they know any local authors or groups you could get in touch with. Facebook and Goodreads both have lots of online groups for writers of many different genres.

It is true that there is safety in numbers, so finding and working with fellow authors on different projects and ideas can be hugely beneficial for all concerned. And there is nothing to stop you setting up your own group in your area that focuses on your topic or wider LGBTQ+ issues.

Setting up and being the driving force for a writing group does have its challenges and can be extremely time-consuming, but there are benefits in the shared collective and the exchange of experiences such a community offers.

4.3.1 Set Up A Writers' Group

When I first set up an independent writers' group to encourage other authors in and around my hometown to self-publish and market their books, the philosophy was simple: we were stronger as a collective, we could reach more people, and therefore more book buyers than we ever could as individuals. It proved to be a fantastic launching pad for first-time independent writers, and a great source of information for us all. It is vitally important, however, if you are setting up such a group, to establish what you want to get from it at the outset. You must set the rules first.

Here are a few things to consider:

- What is your group about? Are you going to be LGBTQ+ exclusive or open to everyone? Nail what it is your group is going to offer to its members and what it is going to do for them. Are you going to meet once a month in a local pub and talk about your latest projects for some friendly feedback? Are you going to have a stall at the local market once a

fortnight? Do you intend to give library talks to the public? Think very carefully about your plans going forward and get everybody on board. Write a constitution and get everyone to sign up to it.
- Engage with writers who have the same vision as you. You need to have a plan of where you want to be, both as a group and individually, in one, two, and three years' time, and that means asking each of the members to state their ambitions too.
- Each member of the group must contribute the same level of enthusiasm and effort into reaching the groups' constitutional goals. It will seem like you're running a small business, having to deal with personnel issues as well as venues, suppliers, and accounts, unless you delegate and strictly control who does what and when. Do not fall into the trap of 'its quicker to do it all myself', because other people will let you do just that. Get everyone to commit to doing at least one of the core tasks: running the website, treasurer, printing marketing material, etc. To do these things willingly they will need to feel they have a vested interest in the groups' ultimate success and that they will get something back for their efforts.
- Do not let just anybody into your group. Writers of all ages and persuasions have very different abilities, and what they might think of as their best work, may in fact be so full of errors, both grammatically, and typographically, that to have their book on the same shelf as others, would seriously diminish the entire group's reputation. Get rid of those people quickly, but be gentle, you don't want them bad-mouthing you or your group.
- Everybody will bring different skills and something unique to the table. It is your job to try to fit them into the group so that they work cohesively for the

greater good. It is not a simple task and does take a lot of diplomacy and management skill. If that's not your bag, identify someone in the group who is a natural leader and seek their advice or better still, get them to do the job of 'manager'.

The group I set up had all these problems, but all the good things too. When we first started, we never envisaged just how quickly it would grow, and how successful it would become. We had no definitive plan or goal, all we knew was that there was some local interest in self-publishing – at our first meeting we attracted four other writers. For a small Cathedral town of 23,000 inhabitants, the fact that we quickly grew to an average meeting of 20 authors from the surrounding area, seemed quite incredible to us.

After a few months, we applied to become a CIC. This entailed a long application to the Office of Community Interest Companies, but as a successful group, with a commitment to social and community goals, being a CIC meant access to certain benefits. For instance, people can donate knowing that there are protections in place to ensure that any funds raised are only used for stated purposes. It also provides limited liability, giving protection against individual libel. You will need two named persons to act as directors.

Being a CIC gave us prestige as well. We positioned ourselves not only as a writers' group, but as an active community group with a collective voice that people listened to.

After about two years working hard for the group, my enthusiasm started to wane. At the same time, I was trying to maintain my own writing. My energy and my vision of where I wanted the group to go started to fade before my eyes. This was my failing in not establishing the group's goals at the very beginning. The effort I was putting in was not reaping anymore rewards, especially in terms of book sales. It was the same ones doing all the work, while others wised-up to the best events to get involved in and opted out of those less lucrative, and despite us vigorously trying to explain otherwise, new people joining seemed to think that the group was there simply to do things for them. We were nurturing new authors rather than moving forward as a group. In the end there was no momentum, it was simply becoming a rote of stall holding.

What I missed when I left the group was the camaraderie and the support network it gave me. But it is clear, it's not enough to just surround yourself with like-minded, supportive independent authors, it is a question of the direction you want to go in that's the important thing.

5. Getting Expert Help

Now that you've committed to telling your LGBTQ+ story, all you need to do is get going with the writing, and keep at it until it's finished.

But let's take a moment or two to think about some of the potential pitfalls you could encounter in your eagerness to get to the end and get published.

- **Not getting your book professionally edited and proofread:**
  Whatever your considerations for your book, it is the experience other people get when they read it that will determine whether they remember and recommend it to others, or not. One or two typos in any book, even those traditionally published, is jarring, but can be forgiven. Any more than that is a potential death knell. A good editor, and by good, I mean a professional who is earning a living at doing just that, is vital, and you need to be prepared to pay for it. A school-teacher friend may be able to help you with some proofreading, but they might find it challenging when it comes to LGBTQ+ non-fiction and you might not be comfortable with someone close to you critiquing your life story. Take time to find the right people to work with you, and it will pay dividends.
- **Not formatting your book properly:**
  This doesn't just mean uploading onto a self-publishing platform. That is relatively simple to do. Formatting is how the text on the page looks to the reader. Unless there is a very good reason for it, such as making the text readable for dyslexic people, or you are writing for the visually impaired

or small children, stick to tried and tested approaches. Look at non-fiction books on your bookshelf and you will see a standardised look inside. By not doing so, your book could end up just looking amateurish, and distracting for the reader. You can hire someone to typeset your manuscript for you and this might be particularly beneficial if you are thinking of including images, graphs, or diagrams.

- **Not getting your book cover designed by a professional:**
  As with editing, the design of your book cover is a job that should be given to a professional, and thus it will cost you money.
- **Not budgeting:**
  It is said that self-published authors who get as much professional help as they can afford, especially with editing, and cover design, can expect to make more sales. It can also be quicker to recover costs if you have a catalogue or series of books behind you, as well as a well-supported author platform. However, don't get carried away spending what you cannot afford, be firm with yourself, especially if this is your first book; know exactly how much you are willing to spend and not recover, and stick to it.

5.1 Planning Your Budget

Knowing your budget plan and the amount of money you can afford to lose, is essential.

It is very easy to get carried away, forking out unaccounted for sums of money on editing, proofreading, cover design, website building, book launch events, etc. Before you know it, you have spent hundreds, possibly thousands, especially if you don't keep a close eye on your finances, and properly plan your book's production, launch, and marketing.

Numbers differ wildly about the true costs, but a mooted average production cost to self-publish a book is said to be £440. That seems low to me, and I would suggest that it's nearer £800–£1,000. And that figure doesn't include any marketing or paid advertising you might want to do. Of course, you can do it for nothing if you don't seek any professional help at all.

The Author's Licensing and Collecting Society in the US found that typical returns were approximately 40% of initial investments. Therefore, an outlay of £5,000 for instance, might only return £2,000. When the average full-time earnings per annum for established traditionally published authors is estimated at around £11,000, you can see that over-spending is a dangerous hole to fall into. Spending nothing is an option, but if you have the means, as Joanna Penn, an author-preneur, who has certainly made a success of her own self-publishing career says, 'think of the cost of self-publishing as an investment, and your book as an asset that earns you money long-term.'

Always aim for the highest quality in everything you do, but do not sell your granny in order to achieve it!

What are the absolute must-haves?

- **Editing:**
  This is absolutely a priority for any writer. No amount of self-editing and proofreading by a 'trusted friend' will pick up on things such as structure, flow, legalities, paragraphing, sentence development, typos, and grammatical errors. If you

know someone who has editorial skills and can do this for you, excellent, but for most, this is the number one task that must be budgeted for. Depending on the length of your manuscript, and the quality of your writing, a good editor will cost anything from £300. You might care to look at www.ciep.uk and search 'rates'. Always try to go with someone who has been recommended to you, and who fits your topic.

- **Proofreading:**

  This is something you can ask someone you trust to do who has an eye for detail, a very good knowledge of the English language, and is willing to spend a considerable amount of time helping you out. The difficulty is that, without payment, there is little incentive for a non-professional to get the work done quickly or be 100% accurate. Professional proof readers will cost in the region of £300, dependant on the amount of work they need to do. Again, check out CIEP's website. Always have a proper discussion, and be truthful about the areas of your writing you are not completely confident with. They will require a chapter or two from you to determine the amount of work they think they will need to do prior to giving you a quote.

- **Cover design:**

  Unless you have some experience of book cover design, as opposed to being artistic, which is very different, leave it to the professionals. A cheap looking, amateur attempt at creating a visually stunning cover will be the result if undertaken by anyone, unless they know exactly what they're doing. Front and back cover design and formatting can cost anything from about £250 upwards. Some people will offer to do it cheaper, but do research their previous work first.

(The above three points are covered in more detail in Part Two in the chapters: Editors, Editing, and Proofreading, and Cover Design).

Anything else you do that requires professional help in relation to your book, such as formatting (if this is something you cannot do yourself) or, marketing and promotional materials, will all be expenses on top of these three essentials. So, even now, a minimum of £900 of investment is not an unrealistic figure to launch a professionally produced and finished book, that would have no problem sitting on the shelves of any bookshop. Can you afford that? Can you afford never to see that money come back to you, or at least not for the first year?

If the answer is no, then you will have to think outside the box, and find ways you can compromise to cut costs. Don't be disheartened. This need not be the end of the road for your writing and your dream of publishing your own book. Far from it. But be clear about what you can, and cannot, afford, and use that as a starting position. There is nothing wrong with a meagre beginning.

For instance, if you cannot afford to pay for professional editing, you are going to have to pull in favours from friends, or friends of friends, and put trust in your final judgement and your own editing and redrafting skills. You will have to go through your manuscript meticulously. Consider investing in a book about editing to help you. This way of editing and proofreading your book need not necessarily be a bad thing. People will be forgiving of a few errors and mishaps for a first-time author who has a strong voice, and a story and tone that is clear. They will appreciate that you are self-publishing to help others. They will be less supportive, however, if there are gaping errors on every other page, or a subsequent book you publish which has not improved on the last. Enlisting as many people as you can to read through your manuscript is a way to proofread and clean up errors and typos, and they may also give you constructive guidance on areas for improvement. Take on board what people tell you even if you don't agree, because they are expressing their view as a reader.

With cover design, if you really cannot find anyone of repute at a cost you can afford, you can do it yourself, but get some meaningful opinions on the end result, and only create something that is inoffensively conformist. You will need to be cautious when it comes to uploading your cover design onto your chosen digital platform that your design fits the template parameters properly. KDP does offer a self-made cover creator service.

Think positively and the universe invariably supplies the answer. It will take longer, and mean more work on your part, but rather that than get into a spiral of uncontrolled debt.

When thinking about your budget, think also about where you will be selling your book. If you are selling at bookshops and events you will need some stock to draw from. Don't order too many at a time as paperbacks can deteriorate, especially if kept in damp conditions. Print on demand (POD) services allow you to order as many author copies as you need, and with different delivery charges dependant on how urgently you need them, you can keep a rolling stock at home quite easily, and within a reasonable unit cost. You can also arrange for deliveries to be sent direct to bookshops from your online supplier.

Factor in the cost of review copies and give-aways when making your first order, and look at other books in your genre of the same length to work out the RRP (recommended retail price). Have the price printed on the back cover so that shops and outlets do not have to stick labels on.

Bookshops will require at least 35% discount on the RRP so that they can sell your book and make a profit themselves. It is no use pitching your book at a price that, after taking the discount and your delivery costs away, you start to cut into the cost price to print the book in the first place.

Price your book correctly. Don't be shy about the worth of your writing. Non-fiction books are priced higher than fiction because of the value of the knowledge they contain.

Think about other marketing resources you are going to want once you've published. Business cards, bookmarks, postcards, posters, or any other promotional materials. First, get some costs together from a few suppliers. Does the cost fit within your budget? If you can only afford 500 business cards, work out how many books you need to sell before you can afford a poster and a stand you might like to use on panel discussions or library talks.

Always keep a record of all your costs, your outgoings and incomings, on a spreadsheet, and keep it constantly up to date. You should also include travel expenses, if you're booked to do a library talk in another town, for instance. Keep all your receipts. You may not need to declare anything to the taxman, but it will keep you on top of how much you are spending.

5.1.1 Crowdfunding

Crowdfunding is the practise of funding a project by raising small amounts of money from a large number of people, usually via the internet. It is a popular alternative way of raising capital to support ventures and artistic projects that would otherwise find it hard to get going, and book publishing is one of its major sectors.

There are many different online platforms that offer such services to small start-up businesses, charities and creatives, including artists, filmmakers, musicians, and writers. Kickstarter for example, is easy to get set up on and use. In the ten years since it was launched in 2009, there were 433,000 projects listed on Kickstarter alone. Of those, 11% of the projects submitted were book related. It is the third highest segment below film and music (16% and 13% respectively).

To start, you will need to submit a pitch about your book project, how much you need to raise and what your reward system is going to be. It works by giving people who pledge money to your project different rewards, depending on the amount of money they pledge. The trick is to make the rewards as worthwhile, fun and as unusual as possible, and be relevant to your book.

People who invest in your project will want to feel they are getting something of value back, as well as supporting something they are interested in. A £10 pledge might be the lowest level on your funding scale, but that doesn't mean you simply make the reward as cheap and meaningless as you possibly can. A simple name check at the back of your book might be enough to entice some funders. A signed paperback copy is an idea for the next level, say at £12. Bear in mind that the lower pledges will be the most popular so you will need to think about the unit cost per item, and also the post and packaging you will incur. Whatever someone pledges, £10 or £100, you do not want all that money lost in having to honour the rewards.

Be honest about where the money you raise from your crowdfund will go, i.e. on editing, cover design, or whatever it might be. Above all make sure you do the sums and talk it through with someone who has experience of crowdfunding first to double-check you've accounted for everything and every eventuality.

Crowdfunding can provide new followers for your social media too. However, without a large following in place already it will be difficult to generate organic support for your project.

Going down the crowdfunding route is time-consuming, and produces a lot of added stress knowing that you must reach the target amount. You will need to be on top of your marketing, and make a plan that builds momentum and interest weeks in advance of the project going live.

If your crowdfunding project does not have the 'wow factor' to gain a snowballing of interest, it probably isn't going to be worth your time and effort.

The rules of Kickstarter mean you have to raise the money within a specified time limit, and they take a fee. If you need £5,000, add on the percentage the platform will take away from the final figure you raise, plus the cost of the rewards, and make that figure the sum you ask for.

Crowdfunding sites have huge browsing traffic, so people need something that will catch their attention in milliseconds.

When planning your pitch keep these simple rules in mind:

- Keep your content short. The average successful campaign includes a description of no more than 465 words.
- Book projects seeking to raise less than £5,000 are more successful than those asking for more.
- Include a high-quality video featuring you talking passionately about your project. Projects with videos are 105% more likely to meet their goal.
- Keep your backers up to date and informed constantly. Creators who update their backers at

least every five days can see three times the increase in contributions.

Kickstarter's overall success rate for book projects runs at about 32%. Money pledged is returned to backers if the full amount of the project is not reached in time.

Indiegogo, which has a wider remit including charitable projects and business start-ups, might be good for you if you are thinking about setting up a small publishing company of your own, or have a charity connected to your book project, but the overall success rate is lower due to a wider interest audience. The good thing, with a slightly higher fee, is that Indiegogo will pay out on all funds raised, even if you do not reach your target, which might be a consideration worth thinking about.

Unbound is a crowdfunding site specifically aimed at independent authors. They include in their package, editing and the production costs of publishing a book. They do have a submission process which includes submitting your manuscript for approval.

6. What is Stopping You?

Being an independent author is about so much more than writing alone, and the added stresses that brings can lead people to wonder:

Can anyone be an indie author? Is there a type of person best suited to withstand all the challenges?

Different people fair differently and will be at different stages in their writing journey. Consequently, the obstacles they need to overcome will vary. Some will be happy with what they have achieved in just getting their thoughts and experiences down, and perhaps what they seek is companionship and the camaraderie of fellow LGBTQ+ writers and readers. That is perfectly reasonable. Others might want something bigger for their books.

You might be feeling cautious, not knowing how far you want to take your writing without first having some knowledge of what's involved, but if you think carefully about what you want and where you see yourself being in a year or two, or aspiring to, this will give you a good starting point.

So often people say, 'I'd love to write a book, I've got this great idea, but I don't know how to go about it.' Or they say, 'How on earth do you find the time to write, as well as have a life?' The crux is you are not going to fulfil your dream if you never actually sit down and write, whether in front of a keyboard or with a pen and paper.

Some people who dream of being a 'published author' only really want to write. To them, the idea of marketing, of setting up an author platform, and the time and effort it takes to sell books, is quite unappealing. And that is a totally valid standpoint.

Identifying your goals and aspirations is key to your self-development as a writer.

Also, a common worry is that whatever you know, everybody else knows already. This negative thought can lead to the assumption that we shouldn't even bother writing our personal stories, and is a strong reason why people don't take up the challenge – because they think it's all been done before, or that nobody will be interested or will care.

Sometimes there are imaginary, or seemingly immovable objects and constraints that put a stop to us fulfilling our dream. What is it that prevents many of us from getting on and doing? Why do we procrastinate so much and have such little belief in the fact that we can do something, if we put our minds to it?

It is a popularly held belief that like painters and sculptors, writers are glamorously gifted, and are naturally brilliant individuals who have sharpened their artistic skills through years of polishing their craft, and they have qualifications and Masters' degrees tucked under their belts to prove it, giving them credibility. We think of writing as an innate talent that very few people are born with, and that we are not one of those. By nurturing this delusion, we simply hang on to the dream and never fulfil it. Most people who say 'I'd love to write a book but …' have these feelings of being inadequate and that they are not eligible to be an 'author'. This is nonsense, of course, because, as with any other artform, there is plenty of room for diversity of style and it doesn't mean that one creative person is less talented than the other.

Everyone has to start somewhere. No one came out of the womb painting the Sistine Chapel or writing *Wuthering Heights*.

When you start out, you need a lot of encouragement and support, not the opposite, which can be very damaging and can lead many to give up altogether. Often it is simpler for budding writers not to seek approval, or criticism, from others, and especially for their self-preservation when writing about LGBTQ+ issues that includes autobiographical detail.

If you find you have friends or family members who relish in putting you down when you talk to them about your writing – don't talk to them about it. I am not suggesting cutting these people out of your life, but just don't mention your writing, and turn the conversation around if it comes up. Try to find and share your thoughts on what you're doing with people who will encourage you and who do have positive things to say.

Of course, we need a nugget of interest in articulating our writing and a degree of aptitude, but through repetition, and hard work over many years, the skills needed to be a good painter, craftsman, or writer can be learned and perfected. The point is, not to give up just because someone doesn't think you are worthy of the accolade of 'author' or that they think your achievements are somehow not 'real' because you are self-published, and that you do not deserve the same level of respect as a book written by somebody who just happens to have their book in the window of Waterstones.

Here's what you can do to help allay negative thoughts:

- Have a good work ethic. Put in the hours, and by doing so you will improve naturally through repetitive crafting and practise.
- Get some good books, or do a course that will teach you grammar, technique, and structure.
- Forget, for the time being, the end goal of publishing your book. Think instead in terms of step by step, page by page, what needs to be done each day to get there.

- Write down your worst fears about writing, and also what you enjoy about it and how it makes you feel.
- Convince yourself that actually nobody is going to read your book, and by doing so, release yourself from that obligation, and minimise the importance of it in your head.
- If social media triggers anxious thoughts and darkens your mood, switch it off. Engage with it at a set time of the day when you are not writing.
- Do not worry about what other people think. Good feedback can be another pressure to perform to an ideal, and bad feedback can fester.
- Work out what motivates you and make certain you always move forward in that direction.
- If you think that what you've written is terrible, put it to one side and go back to it a few days later with fresh eyes.

Will I live up to expectations? Will different research I've not come across expose a flaw in my own? Will people like me after they've read my book? All these thoughts will lead to more pressure. Just be kind to yourself and take care how you talk to yourself in your head.

When you get anxious about something and feel you're walking towards the edge of a cliff, tell yourself you will be safe. You will be here tomorrow, doing some more writing, the same as you always do. Nothing is going to change. Your book is not something upon which your life or anybody else's depends on. In the grand scheme of things, if your book languishes unread, nobody will care except you. It will quickly disappear into obscurity. The world will carry on spinning, and you will be free to start writing something else.

If you have a writing regime, a time when you don't look at your phone and you concentrate solely on letting the creative juices flow, don't then put problems in the way. If, for some reason, you can't go online to do research, do some editing, or redrafting instead. If you can't get to your laptop or computer, sketch out some ideas on paper. Use your writing time productively, even if you're not actually writing.

Personally, I do not have a specific timeslot set aside each day to sit down and write, my life doesn't work like that, and I've learned that neither do I. I know the times of the day that best suit me to write and that once I start, I can be at it for two or three hours before I reach my productive and creative limits. Then I need to go away and do something else. My work ethic is to write, do some research, make connections with people, and do some social media every day, in between whatever else is going on in my life. The trick is to keep at it and be consistent.

Remember, too, that a work of art is not art until it is consumed by someone else, and you have no control over that, how it makes them feel or if they ever think about it again. Once your book is completed and published, you do not 'own' it. It is the audience who completes a book, not the author. This is what motivates me onto the next project. As soon as one book is finished, and even before it's released, I'm already thinking about the next thing I'm going to get stuck into.

6.1 Am I Expert Enough?

When writing non-fiction, we can be distracted by a dissenting voice that niggles away inside, telling us that we are not expert enough in the field we have chosen to write in. That voice reinforces concerns we may have that we are not qualified as someone who should even consider writing about something that already has heaps of academia on the subject. Having an interest in something does not automatically make someone an expert at it, after all. We know this and this is what we tell ourselves, and it is what others will tell you too.

You might also validate this by saying that if the book you want to write is not already out there, there is probably a very good reason for that.

In the end, you might think that the world doesn't need or want your book. This is another untruth, because no matter how many other books there are available on your topic, yours will have a unique perspective. No one else will have written *your* book from *your* point of view, and y*our* experience will resonate with readers because of that. The very reason you must write your book is because there is nothing quite like it out there on the market and that is a perfectly good enough reason.

You might also think that your knowledge of the subject doesn't amount to very much, and certainly not enough to fill a whole book. An interesting point worth noting here is that if you have read three books on any subject, it is said that you already know 90% more about it than the average person on the street.

Insecurities about your worthiness to write your LGBTQ+ story can be disguised in spending months and months researching, but never getting to the stage where you actually begin to write your book. Getting stuck in a never-ending cycle of doing one more piece of research, one more book to read, because you don't feel expert enough, and the book you dreamed of writing will never get finished.

The truth is that you do not need to be the authoritative voice of all the experts, or even be one of the experts, to write your inspiring LGBTQ+ book.

The first thing to remember is that many specialists in any given field do not have the first-hand experience in their chosen subject in the way that you do. How many books are out there written by gay dads about being a gay dad? How many books talk about what it's like to work in certain industries or careers, or about sex or disabilities or our place in society, that are written by LGBTQ+ authors? Experts may have read many books, gone to college and university, and studied for years to gain academic knowledge, but they will never have the lifetime of experience that you have. They do not know what it is like to wake up every morning and feel the way you feel with your gender or sexuality and the consequences that brings, as part of their everyday life.

People who look for self-help books do not want to be preached to by experts. What they want is to feel an affinity with the content and that the author understands them and their needs.

Don't feel that it is down to you to write the definitive book on your topic. You might want yours to be the reference book that everybody refers to, but your subject might just be too big, and readers won't thank you for a thousand-page thesis they have to plough through. If you get to the end and you think there is more you want to say, think about writing a sequel, or how about pamphlets that focus on any one aspect? It is better to leave the reader wanting more than to overwhelm them with more and more information.

In your writing, try to balance the use of LGBTQ+ specific language. While it might be proper and accurate, the overuse of 'homosexual', 'transsexual', 'hermaphrodite', and many other Latin-based scientific sounding names, might alienate some readers. Here's where you really need to know who your target audience are so that you use the language that is familiar and appropriate to them. Avoid writing too many colloquialisms or slang and if you have to use swear words because of the context, keep them to a minimum or you will turn some readers off.

If you are nervous about there not being any interest in your book, talk to people you know who are aware of the importance of LGBTQ+ issues, and particularly the ones you want to cover. You will be surprised to find that many of them have been looking for just such a book as yours and they can't wait for you to write it.

6.2 Mental Health

Before we go further, let's take a moment to talk about our mental health.

It is well known that people from the LGBTQ+ community have a higher propensity to suffer with these issues. According to mentalhealth.org.uk, members of the LGBTQ+ community are more likely to experience a range of mental health problems over their heterosexual counterparts in areas such as depression, suicide, self-harm, and alcohol, and drug abuse. A report by Stonewall, based on YouGov research (2018), which included 5,000 LGBTQ+ people from across the country, showed that 52% had experienced some form of depression, that widespread discrimination was a norm in many healthcare settings, and that because of the fear of such discrimination, one in seven LGBTQ+ people avoided seeking any sort of healthcare help at all.

Many people, both LGBTQ+ and heterosexuals, find themselves beaten down by what might be described as 'everyday' fears and anxieties, as opposed to clinical anxiety and depression which can literally stop someone from getting out of bed in the morning or lead their thoughts to very dark places. If you suffer from any debilitating anxiety you should seek professional help, for instance through LGBT Switchboard UK or your GP.

There are things we can do when our worries and concerns stop us from fulfilling what we want to do – the so-called Imposter Syndrome – the inability to believe that our success is deserved, or has been legitimately achieved through our own efforts or skills. Writing our stories down is one method that can help us see our potential and worth, and can give us a sense of perspective: literally, putting some distance between ourselves and the page, so that we see things more clearly.

This not only works on a conscious level as we read back to ourselves what we've written, but also on a deeper, subconscious level, too. Writing has long been linked to enhancing improvement in mood, well-being, and in reducing stress. Putting down our thoughts onto paper helps us to communicate our innermost feelings more effectively, in ways not always possible in face-to-face conversation. Writing about emotions and difficult or traumatic experiences, however hard to do at the time, helps reduce stress and allows for time and space to explore those feelings further. The written word can also be revisited and viewed, often in a clearer way.

What can stop many of us from writing about feelings and emotions is the fear of exposure, that we will unwittingly reveal our hidden thoughts. How do you write about sex, for instance?

It is possible to distance ourselves' while still delivering the truth by writing in an historical context or setting, or by writing under a penname, as discussed previously. Remember that although you are telling your story, it is up to you how much of yourself you reveal. Make it true, but don't feel obliged to be sensationalist by telling the reader every single, intimate detail. Remember also, that writing about our LGBTQ+ sex lives is important to destigmatise what are often taboo subjects in wider society.

A good way to allay these negative thoughts is to be selective about who or what you engage with. Social media is an addictive demon that can sap anybody's positive energy, and easily darken your mood, when it seems that everybody else in the world appears so perfect and happy and fulfilled. We all know that this is not the case at all. It can be easy to get fixated on homophobic rhetoric and hateful messages that slip into our timelines and newsfeeds, or even just political viewpoints that we do not agree with. Limit your time on social media platforms, and instead broaden and stimulate your mind with art, reading novels, going to galleries, theatre, or even for walks in the countryside or by the sea. Talk to people when you go shopping. Interact with the real world and you will find people are kind there.

When I began writing seriously, my aspiration was to produce and publish a novel. That was it, and I reached that goal. It transpired, however, that my subconscious had other ideas. I hadn't a clue at the time, but what I was really writing about was my life experiences hidden in the prose of my fictional characters and unfamiliar settings. On a deeper level and unbeknownst to me, I was trying to make sense of my feelings around my sexuality, as well as deal with unresolved relationships with my mother and father. My subconscious had pushed me to take the first steps on a path of self-help therapy which later resulted in my book, *Gay Dad*. Though this book included the stories of ten other gay men, it gave me the vehicle to tell my coming out story, and it helped me on the journey to come to terms with and acknowledge my sexuality. It also helped me find other gay men in the world like me.

For me, writing has always been a way of cleansing: of clearing out those dark corners of my mind, and it has helped me to understand my life, my purpose and place in the world. I always feel much better for it.

I am not suggesting that if you suffer with acute anxiety or depression that you should not seek professional help, but I am convinced by the idea that writing about your life and your experiences can be dramatically beneficial to your well-being. Storytelling enables us to find *our voice*, and for the LGBTQ+ community this is the most freeing and self-affirming thing we can do for ourselves – finding out who we are, then speaking out.

7. Telling *their* story: Gideon E. Wood

Gideon E. Wood is a writer of 'speculative queer fiction' fleshed-out by his real-life 'Gideonness'. He lives in New England with his cat, but, he says, it's important to know he's not a 'cat person'. He told me about his life, and his writing journey to unearth himself.

I've had a brain inside my head since I was born. It's just the way it's been from the beginning. I was never much a fan of this. Almost certainly, being born queer, and the resulting default 'outsider status', did not do my inner peace any favours. Other factors in my upbringing and makeup also worked against me feeling *a part of*. I could prattle on about that until my nose bleeds, but let's save that for another time and place. For here and now, let's stipulate that, for whatever reasons, my mind was a rough neighbourhood. It was noisy and dangerous. When I was an adolescent, I found ways to quiet the din, to smooth the jagged edges, to cover it all over with dirt. I used whatever I could get my hands on, substances, people, rage, to make my skull more hospitable. A psychologist might call this approach *maladaptive coping*. I called it sweet relief.

The funny thing about minds is they're complete zombie shitheads. They will not die, no matter what you cover them with, or how much. Over the course of a couple decades, my efforts to bury my brain, my very *self*, met the law of diminishing returns. I found I had neither enough dirt, nor enough back to continue the job of shovelling. At the end of it, I was homeless. I was penniless. I ate from the trash. Something wasn't working. I needed relief from my relief. The way I saw it, I had two options. I could continue until I collapsed, quite literally dead, or I could try another strategy for contending with my own zombie. Either was preferable to the status quo.

I chose the latter option. When I say *chose*, I vastly overstate my own wisdom and work ethic. I didn't get a handle on my vices with my own virtues. Rather, it was the virtues of others. It wasn't a choice. I more stumbled into than chose, and whether by dumb luck or grace, found myself getting well. I began recovering. I like to say I began *dis*covering, *un*covering. For those were the tasks before me. I had to dig up my mind zombie, clean him off, shake his hand, get to know him. As it turned out, I started to realise he isn't so bad. At least, he's not the worst.

When I was a kid, I loved to write. This was before I learned to bury, of course. Like addiction recovery, writing is the opposite of burying. It's an excavation: an unearthing of little parts of myself. As a boy and a young man, I plucked these bits out, brushed them off, polished them up, and shared them. After 20 years of vodka and cocaine, it took a long time to remember the joy of this process. When those memories returned, it took longer still to be able to recreate that joy. Years. I was still (and am still) un-burying myself.

You can see this all over my first book, written about five years into my sobriety. This is a purely theoretical 'seeing', because that book will never find itself under anyone's eyes. Never, ever. It was the hottest garbage. I couldn't tell you whether it was a novel or memoir or autobiography. It was all these things, other things, and nothing much. I was relearning the joyful process of uncovering. Because subtlety is rarely associated with the early days of sobriety. Dynamite was my only tool. At first, I only had the layers I'd packed over myself to share and I had to blast away at them to do so. Still, this exercise accelerated the freeing of myself from the dirt. Through writing, I found emotional, and spiritual health faster. My hot garbage had value. Getting it onto the page was necessary.

Having spent 90,000 words, and a good year clearing my throat, I didn't like the voice I heard. I refused to beat myself up about it. I enjoyed the hell out of the practice: the doing, even if the finished product was not particularly good. It was okay to have fun for the sake of fun. I was finding success elsewhere, in my career.

After a stretch of drunken years, during which I was largely unemployable, this felt good. I took on more and more responsibility, in an extremely demanding field. An 80-hour working week was not uncommon. At one point, I was on-call 24 hours a day for nearly a year and a half. I barely had time enough to breathe, let alone write. About ready to throw myself into traffic, I managed to take a real holiday.

I remember the exact moment I decided to write again, a handful of days into my trip. I'd spent a glorious morning wandering through botanical gardens, taking photos, and enjoying the flora and fauna. After my sweaty trek, I lounged in the shade of an umbrella on the balcony of my ludicrous hotel room. On one side of me, the Pacific Ocean rolled until it disappeared. On the other side, across a little cobbled street, stood an open-air bar. A flamboyant bird landed on the railing directly in front of me.

The sounds of the waves met Debbie Harry's alto and the giggling chatter of vacationing gay boys. Delightful music. A foreign sensation fell upon my face. The bird looked at me and seemed to shrug. I asked him, 'What *is* that feeling?'

I determined it was that my jaw had unclenched. I told myself relaxation should not be so novel. I knew I needed to make a career change. That was one thing, but what would I do with the time and the freedom? I couldn't lounge about on balconies for the entirety of the extra 40 hours a week! This was a frightful notion, as working like a dog made me too busy for active alcoholism, I wondered if I would drink with all that free time. A quick cost-benefit analysis told me not grinding my teeth to dust and avoiding cardiac arrest might be worth the experiment. *I am leaving that place*, I told myself.

When I returned home, I set about the leaving. It took some months to find a suitable position in the Monday-through-Friday, nine-to-five category with a hefty, but not untenable, pay cut. To my surprise, I found I could spend the extra 40 hours each week lounging about, just on my sofa instead of a balcony: I don't have a balcony. I needed the rest and allowed myself to enjoy it for a couple more months. I didn't drink and, in fact, I had more time and energy.

While on the couch, I read a lot. I can get into just about anything, in terms of genre, but I have always loved fantasy. A little gay boy coming of age in the late eighties and early nineties *wanting an escape*? Can you imagine? A gay man who came of age at that time with an overdeveloped enthusiasm for recreational drug use *wanting an escape*? Can you imagine? I think you get the idea.

Anyway, a good high fantasy is not only a portal to another reality. The sweep of an epic and magical tale also makes (no points for originality here) a great backdrop for an exploration of the small and human and decidedly non-epic. Done well, fantasy can lift the most intimate, entertaining stories out of the broader, flashier machinery of the plot. Done very well, fantasy tells those intimate, entertaining stories with extraordinary insight. Small problem here: it's not often done very well.

I'm not here to slag off my fellow creators, so I'll leave the writer's name out. But there I was, on my sofa, knee-deep in an epic fantasy, telling myself, *I think I can do better than this*. Even if I couldn't, I knew I'd have fun trying. I'd already determined fun for fun's sake was a worthy use of my time. It had just been a few years since I had any of that time stuff to spare.

I didn't force anything. I'd already largely unearthed myself and had found, despite my best drunken efforts, I was a reasonably three-dimensional person with thoughts, desires, beliefs, emotions, light, and darkness, a human with things to say about my little life. I did some meditating on these things, and allowed the bigger fantasy stuff, the plot, conflict, magic, stakes, politics, mythology, to come to me organically. It came pretty fast, and usually in the blissful liminality between wakefulness and sleep. Into a notebook (truthfully, an app on my phone) these pieces went. Before long, I had the structure of a trilogy.

Today, into that structure, the bones of a story in which a real person in the real world could never live, I'm fitting pieces of my own, complicated self. I don't feel much compelled to share the blow-by-blow of my story with the general public. I'm a gay writer, writing gay characters in a fantasy framework. I'm not sure the ins and outs of my particular gay life are terribly interesting. Besides, the work of recovery presents ample opportunities for sharing my timeline of events with others. Such storytelling is at the heart of our growth. We dig and sift through the dirt, through the things done to us by ourselves and others, to find out who we are under it all. We learn that person, that identity, never needed covering up in the first place.

In my writing, the story is made up. Even that might be taking too much credit. It comes to me at night, the product of unearned inspiration. Whatever their origins, the beginning, the middle, and the end are fake and a good deal of fun. I hope. Within that skeleton, I share my identity, more than my story. My *Gideonness* fleshes it all out. I'm in there, sprinkled into the characters, and the narration. The real me. The middle-aged queer, who's still guy crazy after all these years. The man who, despite first appearances and his mercurial temperament, is deeply thoughtful and sensitive. The dog person who ended up with a cat. The one who, without the help of others, will smother himself in too much of a good or a bad thing.

I'm not sure I have a heap of insight around getting a queer story out and under queer eyeballs yet. I've only come to treat my writing with seriousness in the last 14 months, and I'm about six months away from the release date of the first book of my trilogy. I'm slogging away, editing that. I have a first draft of the follow-up, a solid outline of the third, and a pile of ideas for future projects. Anything I know about independent publishing comes from asking questions and observation. For me, this largely takes place on Twitter. I seek out other writers (particularly LGBTQ+ writers) and watch them, read their stuff, and probe them for their secrets. I'm building a sense of what works and what doesn't.

The self-publishing world reminds me of the recovery world, strangely. Plenty of help is to be had, if only I'll raise my hand and ask for it. In both cases, it takes guts. If I want to succeed, I must swallow my ego, admit exactly where I'm at, and rely on others to show me how to move myself to the next place. I can't own my identities, queer, alcoholic, or writer, without the help of others. I can't unearth my stories on my own.

You can follow Gideon E. Wood on Twitter, Facebook and Instagram @gideonewood or visit his website www.gideonewood.com

Part Two: Your Book

We have talked about what it takes to become a writer, and the best mindset to overcome worries and concerns you might have in making the decision to write your LGBTQ+ story. We've looked at the importance of establishing routine in your day to allow you to write, and given you things to think about like budget and using the expertise of others. You might have also signed up to do a course or read one or two books that will complement your writing skills. And we've taken stock of our mental health.

Now is the time to begin writing; from concept to first draft, editing and proofreading, *Part Two* will guide you through some of the issues and offer practical advice to overcome them. And, to further inspire you, there are more testimonies from other LGBTQ+ people who have written and published their stories.

8. Structuring And Researching Your Book

The physical process of sitting down to tap away on your computer or laptop to write that first page of your LGBTQ+ story should be an easy task, right? After all, don't you simply start at the beginning and let the rest flow from there?

The beginning can be more difficult to pinpoint than you think.

It is true that writing autobiographical non-fiction is, in some ways, less stressful than writing fiction because you are starting from a position of knowledge. You don't have to invent characters and create an imaginative world, plot or scenes; the facts are already there for you, whether from personal experience or through your research. But with non-fiction, when and where to introduce your reader into your story can be less obvious to determine. Do you literally go back to the beginning of time to set the foundations and back story of what is to follow? Probably not. Similarly, an episodic biography of your life from birth, through school, career, and life events, before you get to the point of your book, is not a good idea either. Even though your whole life has been dominated by your sexuality or gender identity, you need to work out the point at which your tale will begin, and that point has to be relevant to the ending in some way.

Think in terms of a pivotal moment when something happened that inevitably made the rest of the story unfold. The moment you were forced to come out, the day you were homophobically abused, raped, dismissed from work, or ran away from school due to constant bullying. Whenever you choose to start, it is those first few pages that will set your book's tone and grab your reader's interest.

Likewise, (and this is a technique used in fiction), in the middle of your book there needs to be a point of no return: when something else happens, which means there was no going back to where you were before. Then at the end: another event which resolves the story with a good or bad outcome.

Much of our time spent on Earth is really quite mundane. We go from place to place through the years, from one relationship to another, be that with loved ones or friends, without really having any plan or notion of the future. That journey is marked by different events, most have no bearing on our lives at all, yet others are more profound. Some of the decisions we make end in blind alleys, sometimes we are presented with stark choices that are life-changing. Just as in fiction where a seemingly insurmountable problem is resolved, so this must also happen in non-fiction.

A book that simply relays the facts ad nauseum will inevitably be a dull read. Find and focus on one aspect of your whole story that binds it together without which there would not be a story to tell. For a gay person this might be coming out, but this incredibly difficult moment is not the whole story. There might be a reason why they were forced to come out, or a reason why they couldn't until something else happened. Whatever 'the story' is, the coming out scene could be a good place to start by telling the shocking reality of that moment. The end then might be a revisit to that time and how things have changed for the good or how the other people involved in that scene have moved on.

In telling your LGBTQ+ story, include only what is relevant to the whole picture and leave out the rest.

Umpteen hospital appointments retold in every minutia of detail will become tedious for the reader, even though each one of those visits was fraught with trauma for you.

Varying the pace, just as in fiction, will keep readers engaged and interested.

There must also be a strong sense of the moral standing of your book, what your audience will gain emotionally by reading it, and the genuine authenticity of the knowledge and research it conveys.

Be vigorous with your self-editing. Don't add scenes just because they are visually interesting. If it doesn't add to the forward motion, leave it out.

Structuring your book is an important part of its creation. It will help you focus on specific areas and a good structure will engage your readers in a cohesive flow that makes sense. Think of your book as a two, or three-part play where each part is clearly defined, where one follows another in a logical sequence. The length of your chapters or the number of chapters in your book is not set by any rule, but try to keep parts and chapters approximately equal in length.

There are some standards, however, that do work well for readers. Most people do not have enough hours in the day to spend time reading a whole book in one sitting. Life is just too busy for that, and some read slower than others. Keeping your chapters to a reasonable length, therefore, enables the reader to feel comfortable and that they are moving towards the end in manageable chunks. A few pages before bed, or while commuting on the train to work in the morning, might be all they can manage in one go, so having chapters that reflect that timespan is helpful.

A non-fiction book of 250 pages long would not be an unreasonable length. If it's too short it will feel flimsy and perhaps not worthy of the knowledge it contains. Decide if you are going to split your book into parts, then how many topics, and therefore chapters, you are going to have in each part, and establish an approximate page count for each chapter based on your book's overall length.

Map out the structure of your book on a large sheet of paper, or many sheets of A4 paper taped together. It will help you to visualise and control what could otherwise turn into a burgeoning project that is difficult to manage.

Write down the main topics in the centre of the paper and draw branches coming off them for different themes. Write down all the facts you know about each of these topics around the sheet. Exclude your personal experiences at this point. This will give you clear ideas for chapter headings and recurring points of interest. Add your personal experiences. Does this throw up other ideas for further chapters or sub-chapters? Write down any points you need to investigate and questions you don't know the answers to. This will help form what you need to research. You can add more information to this sheet as you build the structure. Add pictures and references to TV shows and YouTube documentaries. Think in terms of a television detective programme where they have a murder case study board with lots of different pieces of information all linked to the central prime suspect.

Once you have your framework mapped out, it is much easier to jump in and out when you're writing and when the time suits you, to add facts and related information of interest as and when they come up.

As you begin to write your chapters, think about using sub-headings within them to make it easier for your reader to find exactly what they are interested in. People read non-fiction in an entirely different way to how they read a novel. Instead of starting at the beginning and reading through to the end, when people pick up a non-fiction book, the first thing they do is flip through it to see what catches their eye, often getting side-tracked in reading a paragraph here or an entire section out of sync. They might go straight to the contents page and start with the topic or issue they are most intrigued by. This is perfectly normal and the more you can encourage this flipping behaviour the better. The perception of the reader will be that there are lots of things of interest in your book for them.

Here's how you can encourage flipping behaviour:

- Don't make chapters too long.
- Split chapters by using sub-headed sections, no more than a few pages long.
- Add case studies or interviews.
- Use check lists with bullet points.
- Highlight important text.
- Include practical tasks and exercises.
- Include links to websites.
- Use easy to read graphics and pictures.
- Have clear resource and citation notes.
- Include references, bibliography, and an index.

Keep an ongoing list of your research including where it was sourced. The internet makes research quick and easy to do, but it also means it is just as easy to forget where a piece of information came from. Always double-check facts by finding different sources and if possible, go back to the original evidence if you can. Wikipedia is a fantastic resource, but it has its flaws.

Investigative research might take a little bit of organising: emails to institutions, and trips to hunt down handwritten letters and original documents or photographs, but the end result will resonate with accuracy and ensure against defamation of character or libel.

How much time should you spend on research?

There comes a point when your story needs to be told and you have to stop poring over more and more research material. Too much information and investigation can suffocate what it is you are trying to say, and the over emphasis and examination of research might add nothing new. Stick to your map and the areas and themes you want to cover and don't get distracted by some exciting new detail that you then spend hours researching which is actually irrelevant.

What is important, is how you are going to weave your personal story through your book.

When we recall one or two of our favourite books, we remember them for only a few things: in fiction it might be a particular character, place or scene, in non-fiction it might be the central voice and the empathy we felt towards the narrator or the revelation of something incredible we didn't know before. Whatever it is, we only remember those books for just one or two paragraphs of writing which conveyed something that made a lasting impression.

The advantage you have is your unique angle from which to tell your story. Work out what that is, and you are halfway there.

8.1 Conducting Interviews

You may want to include other real-life LGBTQ+ experiences in your book. A varied perspective on your topic will definitely help to strengthen and support your message. Other peoples' stories will also add different viewpoints and a humanity to the themes you want to cover. It may be that you simply cannot write the book you want to without the assistance of others and interviewing strangers or even people you know, might not be something you've ever done before, or only in a formal job-seeking setting.

What is the best way to go about setting up an interview? What questions should you ask, and what format should you follow? Unless you are interviewing a politician on television with a limited timeslot in which to get a set of crucial questions covered (without them ducking the answers), an interview where you want the interviewee to tell their personal story should be conducted in a relaxed, informal, and conversational setting. The best interviews are those in which the interviewee reveals their innermost thoughts and memories, with a few riveting anecdotes thrown in. People generally love talking about themselves and their experiences, especially if they feel it will help others too. You might be giving them the first opportunity they've had to tell their story properly.

Here are some tips on how to create the ideal conditions to help your interviewee open up:

- Make them feel comfortable and relaxed. Conduct the interview in a safe space for both of you. More and more interactions are happening via Zoom or Skype these days, but if you are meeting them face-to-face, make it a public place, like a café or bar, but in a situation where you won't be interrupted, disturbed by noise, or be overheard. Remember the sensitivity of the subject area you will be covering.
- Coffees should be on you (a small token of your gratitude to them). You could also offer them a signed copy of your book when it's published. If they ask whether there is any monetary payment, state quite clearly at the outset what you want, and what you will give to them in return. Be very clear and put it in writing if necessary. Most people are very happy to talk and give of themselves freely, but don't be upset if they ask whether they will get paid or not.
- Give them some kind of editorial say on the results of the interview before it makes the final draft but be clear about what that is. Whatever editorial amendments you allow them, you don't want them

to change the tone or nuance of the interview. You want to give them the confidence that you're being open and honest with them, and that you have quoted them correctly, but not give them so much leeway that they feel they can rewrite the whole interview if they want to. If there is something that they really want to change, but which you feel is important to the interview, try persuasion by reiterating the purpose of your book and who you want it to reach. If that fails, pull that question or section out.

- Get to know who your interviewee is. Find out as much as you can about them: Google them, read their blogs, and look at their online presence.
- Always record the interview if you can. It will make transposing and editing laborious, but you won't forget any key points. Confirm with them that they are okay with this. Take a few notes and the odd keyword you might want to come back to or a follow-up question on something they've just said, but make sure you engage with them and look them in the eye. Do not be furiously scribbling away, as this will just be a distraction.
- If you're doing the interview over the phone or via an online video call, make sure they're ready and comfortable before you start, and that there are no background distractions.
- Start the interview in a convivial way. Chat about the weather, how they managed in the traffic, etc. Keep it friendly while you both settle into the surroundings, or while you're waiting for the coffees to arrive.
- Explain and remind them what your book is about, their contribution to it, and what you hope to achieve with it.

- Ask them if they mind their full name being used or just their first name, or would they rather anonymity? This should be established before the interview, but it is worthwhile confirming this again on the day. You do not need a signed non-disclosure agreement, but if you feel it would make your interviewee more relaxed, it might be worth considering. If you are interviewing a group of people in the same room, such an agreement will ease any confidentiality concerns.
- Before the interview, write down what your goals are. What do you want to get out of it? What are the themes you want to cover and what questions do you want specific, factual one-word answers to? Try to ask questions that you have never asked, or heard asked, before.
- Know as much as you can about the latest news and any controversies that surround the topics you're going to cover.
- Keep the interview spontaneous and real. Have your questions to hand but leave plenty of room to allow them to tell you other things that might be invaluable.
- Give them space and time to answer the questions. Don't fire questions at them. You are aiming for a free-flowing 'conversation'.
- Have half a dozen crucial questions plus a selection of others that are less important and will be good to use if you've got time. If the conversation veers off course be ready to bring it back on theme with one of those questions.
- Don't hand your list of questions over before the interview. You want spontaneity, not well-practised verbatim. An outline of the topic, the areas you want to cover, and the crux of what you want from the interview should be sufficient. If they won't do

the interview without a pre-prepared list, you might consider if it's worth doing at all.
- Make the first question something easy for them to answer, and that makes a connection between you both and your LGBTQ+ backgrounds.
- Avoid anything you know will be too tough to answer or personally sensitive. Let them lead the conversation in that direction themselves if they want to. If you really want to delve, wait until much later in the interview and give them the opportunity not to answer if they so wish.
- Ask open-ended questions rather than closed ones, i.e. 'When' and 'how' or 'tell me what happened when …', rather than questions they can answer simply with a yes or no.
- Often people will use the words they really mean by subconsciously hiding them in a sentence. Bring them back to that word or phrase that stands out, 'What did you mean when you said …', or '"duped" is an evocative word to use. Why did you use that particular word?'
- Use the power of the pause to get more out of them, especially if you feel you've heard the same answer before. People feel an irresistible urge to fill awkward silences. Don't use this technique too often though because it will sound like you've got a hidden agenda.
- End the interview with an off-the-wall question to reveal a bit more about their personality. 'What was the last music you heard in the car?' or 'What's your favourite Disney character?'

8.2 Finding Your Voice

How do we find the right writing voice to help tell our LGBTQ+ story?

This might not be something you've considered, but when writing, whether we know it or not, we write in a subtle nuanced voice. As well as establishing a strong story, a well-defined lead character will resonate with your reader in the same way any hero in fiction does. Before you start anything, you need to decide the character you are writing as and the tone that will bring to your book, and to write from that point of view. Are you going to portray yourself as a swash-buckling hero, a wise mystic, or a bouncy, bumbling, loveable clown? You might not recognise or associate yourself with any of these traits, but a different facet of your personality might be the best voice to tell your story.

Be mindful though that our personalities are many layered and we show the world different aspects of ourselves in different situations: at work, at home, on the football terrace, on the dancefloor, to our gay friends and to our non-gay friends. The character you portray in your book should also be multi-faceted and interesting. Your reader will want to get to know who you are, and they can't do that if the only version you show them is the one chasing down corporate executives all the time like an activist on a mission or someone in tears on every page.

While this book is not about creative writing, it is worth bearing in mind how interesting fictional protagonists are created by authors in order to build interest, jeopardy, and bring their characters to life. When it comes to writing your story, remember that main character is *you*.

It can be difficult to get it just right, but humour can also play a positive part in your writing, especially if it is self-deprecating and used to offset scenes of trauma. Try to steer clear of sounding too boastful or talking continually about your successes; how you got a standing ovation at an important LGBTQ+ rally which you just happened to turn up to, or how the whole top deck of the bus cheered when someone said, 'Look who it is!' Although for comedic effect, such scenes could work well, and of course you should tell your readers about your successes, that is part of your story, but keep to the facts and not embellish them with exaggeration. Don't hide important details under too much humility either; that could be construed to mean you're looking for compliments or that the point you are trying to make will simply get missed.

Similarly, it is not a good thing to overwhelm your reader with too many scenes of violence and suffering. When we read, we empathise with the characters, and imagine what they are feeling, in the same way we do when we look at art, a photograph, or a film. It can feel very real to us. In such cases, let the reader imagine what is happening rather than tell them every gruesome, disturbing, detail.

It is difficult sometimes to emphasise and describe to non-LGBTQ+ people what we experience through our lives and have to withstand on a daily basis, and it is important we try to give those readers a deep sense of emotional connection and empathy. Good writing with a strong voice is what gives realism to a story.

It is no good trying to invent someone you are not to tell your story, but identifying different characteristics within yourself will show the reader who you are. Remember, they will not have met you or know anything about you until they turn that first page.

9. Telling *their* Story: Curtis Chin

Curtis Chin is a documentary filmmaker. He lives in Los Angeles.

The eighties and early nineties were a pivotal time in Detroit, both for the city and me. While the US auto industry was collapsing, murder and crime were on the rise as AIDS and crack devastated parts of the city. I grew up amidst all this chaos, trying to figure out my sexual identity, as well as my racial awareness in a city defined as Black and White.

My parents had six children, seven, if you include our popular Chinese restaurant. Located in the city's most crime and drug infested neighbourhood, our family business kept us all busy. It required so much attention that we were there as much as 80 hours a week, cooking, cleaning, and serving endless bowls of wonton soup.

While some might call this child abuse, it was actually a pretty cool childhood. Not only did I get to grow up surrounded by the love of my family, but I got to eat whatever I wanted, whenever I wanted. From the moment we arrived, I usually had a fork, spoon, or pair of chopsticks stuck to my face. It's probably why I was such a chubby kid.

I also got to meet so many different people who came into our Asian-themed dining room for some good food and conversation. The diversity of our customers represented the entire city – black and white, rich and poor, Christian and Jew, gay and straight. We took anyone's money.

Through observation, osmosis, and a sit-down lecture or two, the restaurant was the setting for my greatest education. I learned so much about people, as well as myself. It's where I first explored and nurtured my identity as a queer Asian American.

While I learned so much working in our family business, one thing missing was good literature. The only reading material to be found in our dining room or kitchen were our menus, the discarded newspapers left behind by our diners, or the Yellow Pages. There were no copies of Shakespeare, Marquez, or Mishima lying around.

That's why my parents were caught off guard when I came out to them... as a poet and writer. Like most parents, they were concerned about my future. They asked, 'When did you realise this? How long have you known?' Followed by, 'Do people make any money doing that?'

In truth, I, myself, was surprised about my career path. Majoring in writing wasn't something I was planning to do when I first entered the University of Michigan. Like most first-generation college kids, I was more practical. College was about setting myself up for a good-paying career. It was the era of the hit TV show, *L.A. Law*. I was studying politics and economics with thoughts of becoming the next partner in McKenzie, Brackman, Chaney and Kuzak.

However, during my third year, I started working at a hip diner on campus full of goths and bohemians. It was a fun place to be and so different from my more conservative upbringing. All of our customers, as well as my co-workers, were aspiring somethings – dancers, singers, actors, comic book artists. Since I wanted to fit in with my new circle of friends, I needed to have an artistic pursuit, too.

The expected choice would have been something in the visual arts, since I did show promise as a kid, winning awards and even having one of my pictures included in a calendar from the school district, but pursuing an art major was expensive and I was already on a tight budget. So, I chose writing since it only required a pen and paper, and I could do it almost anywhere.

Taking my first creative writing course was a revelation. I had never participated in a writing workshop before. Even the class size and structure were surprising. Each workshop included twenty students who met twice a week where we sat around a room, reading aloud our own writing, and then nervously waiting for the other writers to critique our works.

In general, my classmates seemed to fit a similar profile. They were white, female, and often middle to upper middle class. Judging by the love interests in their writing, they were also straight. Despite me being the complete opposite to them in every way, I enjoyed hearing their works. It offered me a further glimpse into their lives.

When it came time for me to read my writing in class, I was always scared and uncertain. The things I wrote about were so different from what the others were sharing or discussing. I would get sweaty palms and my heart would race. All these doubts appeared in my brain. What were my classmates thinking about me? Were my stories interesting enough?

My classmates were very open about their past and the struggles they were going through – child abuse, eating disorders, suicidal thoughts. Since I admired their bravery and passion, I decided that it was only fair that I followed suit. I pushed myself to grow. I started to use my writing as a way to address my sexual identity, naming the past boys I had an unrequited crush on. Writing became part of my coming out journey.

In discussing their own works, the other writers also referred to the literary heroes who inspired them. Since I didn't grow up reading much in our restaurant, most of the names and references went over my head. I would jot down the writers and titles and run to the library after class and educate myself.

To help boost my confidence and sense of belonging, I started my own reading collection. I began by asking my classmates for any recommendations. They were happy to oblige with names like T.S. Eliot, Sylvia Plath, and Adrienne Rich. For the first time in my life, I checked out books from the library that weren't assigned in class. I was actually reading for fun.

After ploughing through dozens of titles, I realised that while my list included a couple of gay writers like Walt Whitman and Frank O'Hara, it wasn't very racially diverse. None of the works were by people of colour, let alone Asian American.

Once again, I started to doubt the importance of my voice. Was I saying anything interesting or important? Would I find an audience? Then it hit me, those were the exact reasons I should write – because no one else was writing those stories. It was important for someone to shed light on those experiences.

Eventually, after graduating and moving to New York, I was able to find a community of diverse writers who encouraged me to pursue my voice and hone my vision. Professionally, I've won awards for my poetry, plays, and films. I've written for American television, and I've been able to travel to over a dozen countries in Europe and Asia to present my works.

My current project, *Everything I Learned, I Learned in a Chinese Restaurant*, is a memoir about growing up in my family's restaurant. Told in three sections of eight stories each, it charts my growth from middle school to high school and on to college. It deals with the coming out experience, as well as being an Asian American in a racially polarized city.

Because I grew up as a multiple minority based on my race, class, sexual orientation and religion, the book necessarily deals with intersectionality. It also talks about family, with a mix of Motown, Chinese food and eighties' nostalgia thrown in.

Thanks to AIDS, when I was growing up, I really didn't think I would live past the age of 30. I thought everyone who was gay would automatically contract the disease and die within a month. Luckily, I was able to survive that scare.

Though my readers will most likely not be gay or Asian or even from Detroit, I want to share my experiences as a way of connecting our worlds, to show, that despite our unique lives, we have much in common.

Like a big Chinese buffet, I hope people will sample as much as they like.

Curtis Chin can be found on Twitter @curtischin

10. Seven Basic Storyline Plots

When telling your LGBTQ+ story, think of it in terms of being a good read.

In fiction, there are seven basic storylines or plots. These same storylines can be transferred to non-fiction writing too to bring it to life. They are:

1. Overcoming the monster: *David and Goliath*. The small battling the giant, is a great archetypal story for non-fiction.
2. Rags to riches: *Cinderella*. Starting with nothing, and fighting against all the odds to gain riches that in the end are more valuable than wealth alone.
3. Inner quest: *Hamlet*. Seek, and you shall find. A story of overcoming demons, or finding peace. Perhaps searching for a long lost relative to know who you are.
4. Voyage and return: *Lord of the Rings*. Life throws up a challenge which means you have to leave your roots, or your home, and go out into the world before returning, triumphant, with a renewed and more fulfilled future.
5. Comedy: *Some Like it Hot*. A series of light-hearted sketches that thinly disguise a profound moral story.
6. Tragedy: *Romeo and Juliet*. This classic storyline seldom has a happy ending, but the reader is rewarded with an unequivocal feeling of empathy towards the main protagonist and the shared pain with the author/narrator.
7. Rebirth: *The Metamorphosis*. Rather than overpowering fears and seeking answers, as in the

quest, 'rebirth' is about changing who you are. Overcoming the restrictions of a disability, transitioning, coming out, all enable a full and purpose-filled life, and a change from being one person to being another.

Don't suddenly change the storyline halfway through. Also, don't be afraid to name the storyline archetype you are using by giving well-known examples, such as:

- Overcoming the Monster: 'I felt like Dr Jekyll finally managing to control Mr Hyde'.
- The Voyage and Return: 'There I was, Dorothy Gale, clicking my heels, and finding myself back where I'd started, at home where I belonged'.

These basic storylines work just as well in non-fiction because the hero is constricted in some way at the beginning and ends up with the prospect of a life where everything is resolved. This makes for a gripping page-turner.

Remember also that setting your readers up to think they know what the ending is going to be, only to discover that it is not like that at all will give them a genuinely satisfying and emotionally rewarding feeling at the end. Once they've turned the last page, they will think about and remember your book for a long time after.

10.1 Using Your Diaries

Can we effectively use our personal diaries in telling our LGBTQ+ story?

In his book, *On The Red Hill*, Mike Parker tells the story of George and Reg, a gay couple who met in the 1950s, a time when homosexuality was outlawed. They moved to a cottage in rural Wales; the same cottage that Mike and his husband, Preds, now live in. The two couples had a close bond, and Mike and Preds cared for the old men right up until the end of their lives.

George kept detailed diaries about his daily life and antics, and passed these on to Mike to do with as he wished.

'He was a rarity,' writes Parker of George, and quotes one of the old man's friends talking about him at his funeral, 'He just stared people down. He was a tough old thing who was always, "Take me as I am", he didn't care.'

Parker poses the fascinating question of why we keep diaries in the first place. Who do we write our memoirs for exactly, even to the point, as George did, of editing segments of his daily life out? Did he do that for his own benefit, so that in his dotage he might sit one day and reminisce on what a marvellous time he had throughout his life? Or is it that by editing ourselves in secret, we do so in the hope that one day someone will discover our words and learn about us and see us in a more favourable light? In that case, is it legitimate to edit out the bits we really don't want people to know? Or, as George did, leave in just enough salaciousness and debauchery to cause intrigue? Maybe it is more simplistic than that and we keep diaries simply to shock, or to finally say the things we couldn't when we were alive?

'Your future self is watching you right now through your memories.' (Aubrey De Grey).

Roger Casement, a diplomat and Irish Nationalist, hanged in 1916 for his part in the Easter uprising, kept two diaries. One, known as his white diary, in which he documented his dealings for the British Foreign Office as a diplomat, notably in the Congo and Peru, and a second, more personal account which included his soliciting of young men seemingly at every opportunity, and in every port and town he ventured to. These are known as the black diaries, and there is still some speculation as to whether they were concocted by the British Government to undermine Casement and bring shame on him at the time of his trial. However, the homo-explicit language, and obsession with size Casement clearly had, together with eyewitness statements confirming that the diaries were written in Casement's hand, suggests that they are probably genuine.

Perhaps this is what lies at the heart of diary writing, that it validates our lives with some meaning and purpose, revealing our hidden selves, the true self we most value and yet at the same time struggle to understand and be reconciled with. Writing it down gives us something real we can look at and when later we read them, we find our personal history whispering back to us.

For most of his life, another gay man, and unsurprising civil servant, George Lucas, wrote prodigiously through the fifties and sixties until his death in 2014, committing millions of words to his diaries of his sexploits with rent boys and shady characters he met in and around London's Soho district. He left the diaries to Hugo Greenhalgh who has been painstakingly editing them into a readable format, but, until Mr Lucas met Hugo, he had no idea that his diaries would be of any interest or value to anyone. Of course, today they are immensely important as historical documents of the time, telling the story of a single gay, white-collar worker, living in London at a time when to be homosexual was illegal.

You too may have a hoard of treasured diaries you have kept from your formative years and want to use as a basis for telling your LGBTQ+ story. I asked Hugo where on earth you start with such a vast amount of handwritten information, a lot of which is inevitably mundane and unusable.

'There's no method to my madness, as it were,' he told me, referring to his work on Lucas's diaries. 'The sheer quantity of the material, 60 or so very sizeable diaries from 1948 to 2009, was the initial issue, and still remains so. I picked a year to work on, which works for serialisation if I'm uploading onto social media, but in terms of a narrative for a book, it's a nut I am currently cracking. I'm looking for one theme, and several stories I can trace over a period of several years to give the reader a sense of starting and finishing with Mr Lucas. I am currently reading five diaries between 1948 and 1952. It certainly is a long job.'

I asked the same question of Ian Elmslie, a cabaret artist and author of *A Marvellous Party*, an autobiographical account of his life and the stars he's met. He said, 'Good question; how do you deconstruct a diary? Initial thoughts are to remove the everyday: 'I had a coffee, I went for a walk', and to pick out the adventures. Always bear in mind your intended target audience, who they are, and what you want them to learn from this. Find the theme, define what your book is about. In my book the common denominator was my show business heroes. You need to find the through-line: what is the journey, what do I want, and how am I going to get there, what are the obstacles?'

Personal diaries inevitably reveal a treasure-trove of information about us and the times they were written. It can be very emotional, even scary to face 'the truth' again, but diaries are well worth revisiting to give that first-hand experience and information: how you felt back then; how the times meant you couldn't say anything; who the people in your life were; how they influenced things for you. Look for your younger self's thought processes between the lines. Was there something that you thought could never be resolved? How did that affect your life? How is your life now? What would you say to your younger self?

11. Editors, Editing, And Proofreading

What is the difference between a copyeditor, a line editor and a structural editor; or a proof reader as opposed to a beta reader? Let's go through them.

In fiction, a good copyeditor will not only tell you where your plot is lacking, and where there are holes and gaps, but also, how they feel towards certain characters, the imagery, the dialogue; and crucially, how it all works together. In non-fiction, a copyeditor will look for the same shortfalls, the flow, the use of dialogue, the style, and consistency, and will advise on the overall structure. They will also check facts they disagree with or question, check spellings, acronyms, grammar and punctuation.

A line editor focuses on improving sentence structure, grammar, voice, and style, a job more associated with fiction writing, but they could be helpful if you feel your writing voice is absent, weak or inconsistent.

A structural editor is someone who will take a raw manuscript, and suggest ways of shaping it into something better, and more coherent. If you are stuck with lots of information, and not knowing the best way to present it without it being dull and monotonous, you might consider employing someone who has structural editing skills.

After the copy editing has been completed, think about utilising a beta reader or group of beta readers. The term 'beta reader' comes from computer jargon, where computer programmers release what they call a beta version of a new programme for people to test. Your beta reader/s should be people who have knowledge of, and interest in, LGBTQ+ issues and ideally be in your target audience. They do not perform the same function as a proof reader, though they may well spot errors, and might be invaluable if they know about HIV, Prep, or transitional hormone regimes for instance. Their job is to read the book from start to finish and to feed back their thoughts and feelings about it, and to note any factual inaccuracies. If you happen to know an English teacher or librarian or someone with the right skill sets you can trust to be thorough and honest, then do use them. However, don't rely on, or put well-meaning friends or relatives, under pressure to do a good job on your manuscript. You could end up disappointed.

A good place to find a beta reader is through your LGBTQ+ community. They usually volunteer their services, although you can pay people to do it and there are many you can source online. Don't overwhelm your beta reader with the whole manuscript in one go and be prepared to be flexible with the time it will take them to do a good job. Give them one or two chapters at a time in the order they appear in your book and work on their feedback while they continue with the next section.

When it comes to typos, be warned; it is surprising how two or three people can look at the same piece of writing and still not pick up on the same error. This is because our brains are conditioned to fill in the gaps. Most of us have been reading since early childhood, and our brains are well-used to seeing lines of text running from left to right. If something is not quite right, the brain sees a corrected version for us so that we don't lose the thread of what we're reading. A skilled proof reader will go through your manuscript with a fine-tooth comb and pick out all the typos, incorrect spellings, grammatical errors, or inconsistencies, such as the spelling of names or places.

You should only use a proof reader once all the edits have been done and you are completely happy that the manuscript is ready.

Your choice of any of these editing professionals will depend on what exactly you want them to do, and how much they are going to charge. Many editors will provide all these skills, and it will be important to establish exactly what they are going to do for you right at the start. If you can, go with good, solid, and reliable recommendations. That is not always possible and, in that case, do your homework thoroughly before hiring anyone. Check out LGBTQ+ resources such as Out On The Page or The Writers' and Artists' Yearbook. Another tip is to look up editors and proof readers whom authors you admire have worked with and have acknowledged in their books.

If you require the editor to compile an index, make sure this is something they are skilled at doing or refer to the Society of Indexers to find a specialist who can help you. This will be an additional cost, and is time-consuming and therefore expensive.

Once you have found your editor, and supplied them with a chapter or two on which they can quote, they will send you a 'contract' which will detail exactly what they will do for you.

This should be along the lines of:

- Your manuscript will be checked and edited from your supplied text to a publishable standard.
- You will be advised on any further work the editor feels is required by you as the author.
- The fee will depend on the amount of work they estimate will be needed, but you should expect this to be in the middle to upper hundreds of pounds, or more. They will quote the number of hours and cost per hour, or some charge by the number of words. Charges may change a little towards the end if they feel extra work is necessary, but they should always advise you of this.
- A good editor will keep you informed of their progress, and will leave it to you regarding decisions about increasing their input.

- The quote will allow for time spent checking and implementing minor amendments by you to the edited text, but if you wish to revise your manuscript after editing, or add further material which requires additional editing time, they will charge. For this reason, ensure that your manuscript is as complete as it can be before you let an editor get to work on it.
- Your editor will tell you exactly how they will edit your book, for example in Word from digital files you supply them, and they will email an edited text for your approval in the form of a new file. The edited document is not the final formatted file ready for uploading, and the font, layout, page breaks, and numbering, together with contents, index, source notes, and acknowledgements, etc., are all things to be done by a designer, typographer, or you.
- Corrections will be shown in 'Comments' or 'Track Changes' features so that you can check what has been changed.
- Editing usually commences after agreement and receipt of full payment. Most editors will complete the work within a couple of weeks.

Do not worry about copyright or confidentiality. Editors are professional people. They will not share any of your content, nor information or documents you entrust to them during the editing process. You will continue to own all rights to the edited text, your original text, and all other material you supply before and after editing.

11.1 Preliminary And End Matter

You may want to consider using other parts that make up a book. They should appear in your book in the order they are listed below.

You don't have to include them all, but these sections can be useful aids for readers:

Dedications

A personal dedication by you, the author, appears at the start of your book after the title page and copyright page. It is an excellent way of making a human connection with your reader. The person or people mentioned in the dedication can be family members, or someone who has been supportive and encouraging to you from the start of your writing. But you could just as easily dedicate your book to a whole group of people; for instance, 'For all gay dads everywhere'. A thoughtful dedication can also spark interest, rather than just saying 'To my mum and dad', you might say, 'To Pat and John'. Immediately, the reader is wondering who Pat and John are, and if they are included inside the book somewhere. The point of the dedication is that the message should be sincere and heartfelt, and it creates attachment between the author and the reader.

Contents Page

Non-fiction books usually have a contents page, including chapter number, title, and page number, as readers like to be able to flip back-and-forth between the chapters. Page numbering should start after the contents page. When formatting e-books, your contents page chapter headings must link to the correct chapters throughout the book. There are plenty of YouTube tutorials that explain how to do this.

Forewords

The foreword is a short piece written by someone who has some personal experience of the subject matter in the book, and who champions and supports you and your book.

If you can get a relevant personality, celebrity, or professional guru with insight into your LGBTQ+ topic to write a foreword for you this will absolutely give your book accreditation and some leverage. Don't be afraid to ask either. The worst that can happen is that your request is turned down with a polite 'No thank you', or they might ask for more information before they agree to do it. Be clear in exactly what you want from them, how many words and what they should say in terms of their personal experience that connects them to your book, and how important they feel the book is and why. Give them a timescale of when you need the foreword back and that you'll keep them updated on your progress and the launch date. You might think about sending them a complimentary copy of the book when it is published. A photograph of the celebrity heading the foreword at the beginning of your book will tempt readers in, especially if it's someone they know. Do seek permission to use a photograph and ask to be supplied with one. You could even invite them to come along to your launch party if you're having one.

Introduction

The introduction is where your reader gets a glimpse of what they can expect from the rest of your book. This is really the beginning, and where you explain how and why you came to write it in the first place. You can tell them a little bit about your background and history but avoid overtelling things to the point that it turns into the actual story. The introduction should just be enough to entice, excite and intrigue your reader.

Do not feel that you need to put together an inspirational introduction on the first day you start writing your book.

Ideally, it should in fact be the last thing you do, because as you write, so your understanding of your book and its message will develop.

The introduction should be personable, but it also needs to perform a task as an understated sales pitch to help sell your book, and the tone in which it is written is therefore vital to get right. People will be drawn to something that sounds familiar, but at the same time promises much more. It should also be short enough to read while standing in a bookshop or browsing on the internet. It should be more than the back-of-book blurb, but two to three pages should be plenty.

To start with, begin by framing your introduction in a broad outline, including the main LGBTQ+ topics and key points you want your potential customers to hook into. Avoid using any details you want to keep for the main content of the book.

Set out a clear explanation of what you hope to achieve with your book and what your objectives, expectations, and hopes are for your readers once they have finished reading it. Highlight what the benefits to them and to the wider community might be; how there is nothing like your book on the market, and that you were looking for just such a book yourself but couldn't find it. Tell them what knowledge, skills, or life-changing affirmation your book will offer them. Don't shy away from the serious nature of your book and your responsibility to tell that story. Don't be vague or disguise the premise in coded language or difficult to understand technical words. Be honest, straightforward and concise about what you have written and why you are qualified with the experience to give them the right answers.

Talk about your life but limit this information so that you don't give everything away. Confess something surprising about yourself that you do not mention anywhere else in the book but has absolute relevance to what you are about to reveal.

Do not be disillusioned in thinking that your book will be for everyone. It won't. Know your audience. Tell them what your book is not about. Don't promise the stars if, at the end, you've not even taken off, or you're only just halfway there. If your book includes interviews, tell them how amazing it was to talk to these people and to realise that you were not alone or the only one this had ever happened to. Give some teasers in the form of questions you know people will be wondering about and promise the answers within the following chapters.

If your book is heavily memoir-based or autobiographical, think of the introduction in terms of a short story that encapsulates the entire saga. If writing about a gay family member caught up in the Holocaust, for instance, recalling a scene of you getting on a train as a small child and your great-aunt breaking down in tears when you pass by smoking factory chimneys, will both set the scene and give a sense of the journey the reader is about to embark on: one child's innocent view of the world passing by the train window contrasting with the horror of the aunt's recollection of what she went through many years before. Come back to this scene in the epilogue to bookend the whole story.

Preface

This is optional. The preface is used to talk specifically about how and why the book came about. This can equally be addressed in the introduction. If you find your introduction is a little too long, then you might think about splitting it into two and utilising the preface to talk about the book, saving the introduction as a way of introducing you to your readers. Equally, you could call your preface, 'About This Book' and it could come before the introduction.

Prologue

In fiction, the prologue sets the scene prior to the story beginning. It is often used to establish an important backstory or location. It is less often used in non-fiction as scene setting can be done in the introduction, but it can be used to bring forward a scene or situation from the book that is of significance to the whole story, something that you really want the reader to remember and think about. Don't repeat the same thing twice though. Only use the prologue if it genuinely adds something of value.

Epilogue

This comes at the end of the book and is where the author can bring the reader right up to date with any new LGBTQ+ legislation or advances in medicine, or what happened to some of the characters mentioned. Writing a book can take years to complete, and the epilogue can be an effective way of keeping your book relevant, as well as a place to add any additional information about organisations you might have mentioned in the body of the text.

The epilogue can also be a place where you inspire your reader and point them in the right direction to investigate further the issues you have raised in your book.

There are several ways to write an epilogue:

- **Where are we now?**
  Having gone on a journey through your book, you can bring the reader up to date on how writing it has been cathartic and introduced you to lots of people who have experienced the same LGBTQ+ issues. You should write this kind of conclusion in the present moment, exactly how things are right now. This informs the reader about what you have discovered whilst researching your book and how that may have surprised, informed and made you

feel. They will see that their life will also be enriched with this new knowledge they have gained. Don't leave anything unsaid. Be absolutely clear, and tie up all the loose ends in these final thoughts.

- **Where to next?**
  Your reader might be so inspired that they want to take what they've learned from your book further. Using this epilogue, point them in the direction of organisations or courses. If you have a separate Helpful Links page, send them there. You might also inspire your readers by updating them on someone you met during your research who has gone on to do something amazing for the LGBTQ+ community. If you've got an idea about writing a sequel, reveal a little bit about that, but only if you are certain you are going to write it. In this type of epilogue you are looking to the future and what that might hold, for the reader, the people you've met while writing your book, and you.

- **The cliff-hanger**
  Your story might not have a definitive ending. It might be that your journey still has a long way to go, that the issues you have been writing about are ongoing and will always be a topic of discussion, as is so often the case for the LGBTQ+ community. Through your book, you may have brought a new voice to the debate, a new perspective, but you acknowledge that the subject will never be closed. Here you can use the epilogue to show the reader that there might well be more on the subject to come but you haven't been able to write it yet. This can be an epilogue full of sorrow and regret, so you will need to be careful that you do not leave your reader feeling disheartened or let down with a negative

update. Think in terms of the dumpf-dumpf cliffhanger of a soap opera. Even though the story so far is as complete as it can be, the reader needs to feel encouraged that one day, somewhere, somehow, the final resolve will be the right and happy one.

The main consideration with utilising any form of epilogue is to think about how the reader is going to feel after they turn that final page.

Appendices

If you have graphs, tables, reports, or lists which you refer to in the main text, and if included, would distract the reader from what they're reading, it is a good idea and makes them easier to study, to put them at the back under appendices. You can say in the text 'Refer to Appendices 1:3'. Items placed here can also be additional in-depth information. Don't feel you have to include extra data, not all non-fiction has appendices, it depends on the tone of your book, and the audience you are appealing to. Too much in-depth academic information can, even if placed at the back, put people off if that's not something they are looking for.

Glossary

You might include a glossary of terms, such as colloquialisms or foreign language translations or technical jargon. Name the glossary in those terms i.e. 'Foreign Language LGBTQ+ Terms Translated into English'.

Bibliography

Having a list of recommended reading is not only useful but helps connect you to your readers and gives information on how to explore the topic further. List the books you referred to in your research by title, author, year of publication, and the publisher. You could give specific page numbers for reference too, if the book is an anthology or history book.

Index

Very often, readers of non-fiction will want to search for something in your book on a particular person, event, or place and will refer to the index to do this. The index at the back of the book gives all the page numbers that one person, organisation, or event, etc. appears on. Indexing is a skill in itself and it is advisable to use a professional indexer to do this for you. Of course, there is a cost involved in that, but start by investigating The Society of Indexers. If you are going to do it yourself, you should not include passing references to places and events, or every single person mentioned, unless they are significant. The index should be meaningful and of use. If you are indexing HIV for example, in Word, go to the Find option in the Editing tab on the tools bar and type in HIV. It will find every time that acronym is used throughout your manuscript. It might be very many times, in which case it is best to break it down into sub-headings, for example, by years, decades, or countries. Do not add page numbers to your index until you are at the very end of editing the final draft. Any slight changes or alterations to the text can easily bump pages forward and therefore everything sequential to that will change.

Source Notes and Citations (also called Endnotes)

In the past, non-fiction footnotes were added at the bottom of the page to show where a quote came from or was the place to add further information or a point of reference. Today, footnotes, unless in high academia, have largely been replaced by endnotes, or source notes and citations. Here you can list where your research has come from, also, any notes about the research that might add something to the text, but which was left out of the main content. You can find standard setting out of citation rules online.

Helpful Links

Do list organisations that can give support to your readers should they want it, with a few words about what each organisation provides. Make sure any links you include work and will take them to the correct website.

Acknowledgements

This is the place to thank everybody who had some influence or helped you in writing your book. It can, and often does, include relatives and other people 'for setting me on the right road in the first place', as well as editors, proof readers, and cover designers. People love seeing their name in the acknowledgements, so do name as many people as you want to. They're more likely to buy your book and recommend it to others if they can see they are named. Do check that they are happy for their name to be mentioned, especially as you might be dealing with sensitive LGBTQ+ issues. You don't want to 'out' somebody unknowingly. You could include a disclaimer stating that 'the mention of a person's name does not imply or assume their sexuality'.

At the end of the acknowledgements, remind the reader to post a review online with a link. Tell them where they can follow and contact you on social media and your website if you have one (again with all the links).

Credits

A more formal written credit should be given to anyone, or any organisation, that has provided professional assistance, images, and quoted material, but if this is a limited number it can be included in the acknowledgements.

11.2 Back-of-Book Blurb

The first thing people read when they browse bookshelves looking for a new book, either in the high street or virtually, is the back-of-book blurb. If their attention is grabbed, they will then go to the introduction for more information.

The 'blurb' on the back of a book is an important factor in one of the seven marketing views required to sell it. It is an advert for what the book is about. A well-structured blurb should be both eye-catching and snappy. It can be tricky to get right, but think along the lines of a film preview teaser.

Here are some tips on writing your back-of-book blurb:

- Give your potential readers the next thing they expect to see after they have viewed the cover and the title. It is vital that these elements are cohesive. They will have instantly drawn a conclusion as to what they think your book is about from the cover, now they need to know what it will offer them. What will they learn and gain from reading it? Think of some taglines, one-line questions, or themes. Put yourself in their shoes by pretending you have no idea what the 200 or more pages of this book could possibly tell you when you feel you know a lot about the subject already. Or perhaps you don't know anything. What one or two things spring to mind that would leap out and grab your attention?
- Write in the third person as if a publisher had written the blurb for you. Try to make it no more than 150 words long. Here's one approach; make the first third, i.e. the first 50 words about what the book is about; the second 50 words about fulfilling the answer to their question, 'What problem will

this book solve for me?'; and the last 50 words about why this book is better than any other in the same genre and why you, the author, are qualified to write about it.
- Include one or two questions, and set them out in bullet point format. The idea is to create intrigue. Mix this up with a few sentences, but keep these short too.
- Use testimonials if you have them (but don't make them up!), and use them only sparingly.
- Make sure the design layout is instantly recognisable, that the subject matter and tone can be quickly and easily understood. It is important that the text easy to read, so don't hide it in a patterned background, or make it difficult to stand out from confusing pictures, colours, or by using unusual and difficult to decipher fonts.
- Place a really good strapline in the centre or other dominant position, and highlight it, so that it is the first thing your potential customer sees and absorbs.

12. Telling *their* Story: Nick Taylor

Nick Taylor is an editor specialising in supporting self-published and independent authors. Here he talks about how he came to be an editor and how important it is to him that he uses that skill to help other LGBTQ+ writers.

I first knew I was gay aged 11. I remember the moment as vividly as if it played out just yesterday.

My junior school had a swimming pool, and once a week we would all troop down to the freezing water. One week, after a lesson, me and Jack were leaving the changing room. 'A cheeky look, just in case,' he nodded towards the girls' changing room. I didn't say anything, I just thought *Why? I had everything I needed here.*

I didn't have the vocabulary for my feelings back then. This was 2001, and although being gay was far from criminal even then, its 'otherness' was still being keenly felt. In fact, it was only the year before that it was decreed homosexuality was not a reason to be thrown out of the armed forces. But, in schools, there was still a silence around it: there was still section 28.

You see, that little piece of Thatcher's government was still left over, and would last until 2003, its ramifications would continue to echo through my adolescence. I wouldn't discover gay nightlife for many years, not because it wasn't there, I just didn't know it existed. What else had I missed because of section 28's stifling of language? Caught, in a twist between growing societal acceptance, and a silence at school. Knowing I was 'other', but not knowing the language to describe it. No support networks, no fellowship.

How different that would have been if only there had been more language. A wall with a rainbow flag. An

LGBTQ+ student group. A library stocked with clearly visible LGBTQ+ books. As writer, actor and broadcaster Stephen Fry says 'If I were growing up now […] I would know straight away that I was gay because the internet lays it all out [and] all [the] extraordinary words that are used to categorise us.' Language is crucial to our understanding of ourselves.

We only need to look at the demonstrations against relationship education, that include LGBTQ+ themes, to understand that this silence in schools continues. This is the effect of section 28, as misunderstandings are allowed to continue. A breaking of the cycle, by a simple picture book explaining that two men can be dads and be a loving family, that introduction to language, is critical to young people's understanding of themselves.

Instead, my first experience of LGBTQ+ reads came in my twenties, as I finally got the language I so needed earlier. Alan Hollinghurst's *The Swimming Pool Library* was the beginning of a journey that I'm still on. Through Becky Albertalli, to André Aciman, and stopping off with so many other authors, gay literature opened my world.

Through these works of fiction, my own story was reflected back at me in a way that was safe. Stories hold up mirrors to our lives; characters highlight aspects of our own lives. Most importantly for me, and I'm sure for a lot of other people too, they show us that our stories are not unique.

In most cultures, stories are passed on through the generations. A collective history is told, and the culture grows. Homosexuality often loses out in this cultural retelling. Each generation of homosexuals exists almost devoid of any interaction with the previous generation: we only need to see the rise of HIV infections at the turn of the millennium, not too far from the 1980s peak, as evidence of that. Why, in such a relatively short amount of time after the original AIDS epidemic, would gay men experience such a catastrophic rise in new infections? One reason, stories are not told.

That lack of cultural storytelling, of passing on our history, is what makes LGBTQ+ fiction, all LGBTQ+ stories, so important. In many cases, certainly in mine, it's what connects gay people, and helps them to realise there are others out there, going through the same experiences: that dangerous mix of emotions and feelings butting up to a heteronormative world that tells you your feelings are wrong.

For me, as for a lot of people, we get our language from books. We get our expectations of the world, and of people, from what we read. If I haven't read stories of coming out, how do I know *how* to come out, let alone the words I say when I do. Interestingly, as I write this, I've been thinking about my comings out, note the plural there, and how the language I have used each time is different. Language has to suit the occasion; to be relatable to the audience. As it was, most of my coming out was done too late: I was far too camp to ever need to come out, and when I did it was no great surprise to those around me!

But that's why fiction is so important to me. It is able to say: you're not alone.

That's the importance of all LGBTQ+ writing. It has, in my mind, two, very different, purposes. I'll talk about fiction as, for me, that was my first exposure to gay writing. Fiction, of course, is there to entertain. The reader wants to go on a journey with the characters, to be taken away from their own struggles and worlds and into the world the author has crafted. Without entertainment, why are we reading fiction?

But gay fiction also has to educate. Not in a formal way, of course. But it needs to explore something of the 'otherness' we all feel, and present it in a way that is real and genuine. It is all too easy for tropes and clichés to be perpetuated when writing characters: stereotypes such as the overly camp girls' 'best friend', or the promiscuity of young gay men, are harmful, both for those in the community, as well as those outside.

In the past, 'gay books' have been read exclusively by gay people. Since a number of gay stories have been made into box office successes, there has been a rise in the popularity of gay fiction. Annie Proulx's short story *Brokeback Mountain* was seen by millions when it was released in 2005, and gives a wider population the chance to see LGBTQ+ representation.

Books have benefited from this. *Call Me By Your Name* being the obvious example. And this is the chance for fiction authors to tell realistic stories about life as an LGBTQ+ person. To tell people that are not part of the community, or have no connections to it, what life is really like.

Naturally, books depicting LGBTQ+ characters are not without criticism. Author Juno Dawson's first novel *Wonderland* was criticised for glorifying underage sex (the characters are of age, they are 17 and 18), and as she says in an interview with Attitude magazine, she believes this is simply because 'these are LGBTQ, rather than cis, or straight characters.'

Overcoming this homophobia and getting stories out there is key to changing the attitudes of so many people.

After university and hopping through a few jobs, it was clear that I wanted to work for myself. The nine-to-five wasn't working for me, and I needed to be more creative. But I have always enjoyed being in the background. Behind the scenes, if you will, and I came across an advert for proofreading and copyediting training.

This was ideal for me. My earliest memories are of reading, and to be able to be involved in the process of bringing books to life seemed like the dream job. Through supporting authors, particularly LGBTQ+ fiction authors, to write their stories, I am helping bring about that language that was so absent in my own adolescence.

And that's where I, as an editor, like to work. With books that challenge our perceptions, that ask questions of the reader. I've always seen my job as super-privileged: I get to read stories before anyone else does. And I'm always super-excited when those manuscripts leave me wanting more: when characters really speak to me, or when plots are so well developed, they feel like your own story.

Frequently, editors are portrayed as people who simply spot spelling mistakes and apostrophe blunders. We are more concerned with the finer points of crafting a story. The readers are at the forefront of the editor's mind. As the excellent article in the *Writers' and Artists' Yearbook* says '[e]diting involves refining your writing to make it as readable as possible.' This means focusing on all the elements of your story and getting it to the best possible state before you publish.

Language is the only way authors have of connecting to readers, and when used right, can be incredibly powerful. I'm sure every LGBTQ+ person has a tale to tell of when language has been used against them. Now, writers have more and more opportunities to reclaim that language, and use it for good. Self-publishing, in particular, has opened access to publishing, and for many more people to tell their tales.

And my own language has grown and developed as I've edited. I've been privileged to work with an incredibly diverse group of authors, all of whom have taught me something about language and their own heritage. It's impossible to write anything without your own experiences coming through on the page. In a relatively short amount of time, language around non-binary, trans, asexuality, and pansexuality has grown, and become widely used. The challenge, as always, is to use it right. To inform as well as entertain.

In the foreword to Merle Miller's *On Being Different*, author and editor Dan Savage says: 'That's what the LGBT movement is at its core: people standing up for themselves and their friends and lovers and all the LGBT kids out there; LGBT people facing down the liars, and confronting the bullshit.'

That 'bullshit' is easily perpetuated by writers, even those who are members of the LGBTQ+ community, so it's crucial that we use our language wisely, getting professionals in to support and improve our manuscripts so that we can accurately tell our stories.

Nick Taylor can be contacted via his website www.justwriteright.co.uk and can be found on Twitter @NickTedits

13. Cover Design

Authors these days are expected to write, and edit, their books to a high degree, to work hard on their social media, and to promote and market themselves and their book. The independent author is also the person responsible for their book cover design. While it certainly is possible to create a good non-fiction book cover yourself by sticking to styles that have gone before, if you want something that stands out and has originality, doing it yourself is probably not the best option.

None of us can be experts in all the skills required to produce a book from start to finish, including cover design, unless we have been trained to do so. We have already discussed the importance of professional editing and acknowledge that we can do some of the work, and it certainly helps if we have a good idea about how we want our book cover to look. But the finished article, as with editing, should, if possible, and the budget allows, be done by an expert.

Of course, part of the dream of publishing is an image in our minds of how we think our book will look. It is, after all, the visual accomplishment of all our hard work and commitment, so it is not surprising that it holds such important significance to us in our book's realisation. There is nothing quite like that moment when we open the box on the first delivery and see real books we can touch and hold. But, having a strong visualisation or set idea of how your book should look without at least doing some research, can prove to be a big disappointment or at worst, turn out to be the thing that puts people off buying it.

Having a well worked out design brief will enable a graphic designer to fulfil your wishes, or to tell you that what you are proposing simply won't work for a book such as yours. If you are paying for professional advice, you need to be able to trust their judgement.

Cover design for non-fiction is different to fiction, in that the message being conveyed is not about an aesthetic sense of the story inside. Instead, your cover must tell your readers exactly what your book is about. A good starting point is to emulate what already works well in your genre and not attempt to reinvent the wheel. Look online at similar LGBTQ+ non-fiction books to yours. What are the commonalities? Aiming at the LGBTQ+ market, means that rainbow colours or a rainbow flag somewhere in the design is an instantly recognisable symbol for anyone looking for LGBTQ+ books, but that doesn't mean it is mandatory and you don't want to alienate part of your potential audience by making your book look like it is only for LGBTQ+ readers, (unless it is of course).

Nobody wants their book to look like all the others on the shelf, and the skill of a designer is to get your book to catch the eye of a potential reader for all the right reasons, and not for the wrong ones.

A case in point was the vision I had for my book *This Forbidden Fruit*. I had an idea of a night-time city landscape with light-flare images of people on the streets. In my head it looked amazing, but it was quickly pointed out to me by my designer that this would be too obscure for browsing purchasers to instantly recognise what the subject matter of the book was about. I had to agree, and I handed over the project completely to my designer who came up with a striking, and instantly recognisable, LGBTQ+ cover which works brilliantly. Another good idea is to look for LGBTQ+ book covers that you like, and to look those designers up on Google, (they will usually be acknowledged on the back cover).

If you have a flair for design, and you are willing to take negative criticism, you could design a cover yourself. Non-fiction is slightly more forgiving than fiction, and by sticking to the factual it is much easier than trying to be imaginatively creative. There are also sites where you can look for cheap cover designers but that does come with some risk. Do they look professional? Is the price structure clear? Are the testimonials believable?

The overall perspective of your design should incorporate bold, eye-catching colours, be interesting, and use fonts that are different between the author name and the book title and that do not get lost in the design. The main image must reflect the content of the book but it can be abstract. Also, consider the colour palette and what colours best reflect your book's topic.

When we choose a book off the shelf, we might do so because we know the author, but even then, the front cover can win us over or just as easily put us off through nothing more than a fleeting glance. If we like the cover, a second or two later, we turn the book over to view the back cover and read the blurb. In doing this we take in the continuity of the design and what it, and the words are saying. It all has to make sense to us before we make the purchase.

It is important that, once you have found your cover designer, you explain exactly what you envisage and your target audience. Some designers will provide a crib-sheet for you to fill in. Try to elaborate on that and give them as much information as possible, even examples of book covers you like that are similar in style to what you have in mind for your own book.

Your designer will normally send you two or three variations on the design brief from which you can decide the best and make any tweaks. It might be that you love one image but prefer the font used on another. This is the time to work through such amendments.

Once you have your final PDF copies of your e-book and paperback covers, you are now ready to upload your book onto your chosen digital platform.

14. Formatting And Uploading Your Book

With self-publishing, especially if this is your first time, I would recommend sticking to one easy route to publish your book. In time, you will learn and discover that there are different platforms you can use to reach different markets, but if this is your first foray into the world of self-publishing, keep everything simple and manageable and you won't go far wrong.

When it comes to formatting your manuscript, in other words how it looks in book form, stick to what works. Copy other books you admire and specifically other LGBTQ+ non-fiction books. If you really want to go against the standard forms of layout, font and formatting, and be alternative, you will inevitably put off some of your potential readers. People need to feel visually comfortable. It is therefore better to stick to what is generally regarded as safe and easy for the reader to navigate, rather than try to be trail-blazing and run the risk of disengaging with people before they've even read a word. It is important not to give the impression that you are anything less than professional.

Here is an example of standard Word formatting ready for publishing:

- Times New Roman typeface 11pt.
- Paragraphs are Justified, Body Text, Indentation Left & Right 0cm, Special: First Line 0.5cm, Spacing Before and After 0pt, Line Spacing: Single. 'Keep lines together' un-ticked.
- Chapter Headings centre 18pt, Sub-headings centre 14pt.

- For e-book chapter links, use Heading 1 and Heading 2 for sub-headed sections and Heading 3 for further sub-headings.
- Paragraphs should always be indented, except for the first paragraph in each chapter or sub-section.
- New chapters should always start on a fresh page. There is nothing to be gained in trying to save on the printing costs of a few extra pages by having one chapter immediately follow the previous one on the same page.
- There is no convention for this, but page numbers centred at the bottom of the page feels right.
- At the end of the book, but before Appendices, centre the symbol ~ (tilde) to signify The End of the main text.
- For non-fiction, white paper (which is cheaper) rather than cream coloured is generally the norm.

As a rough guide a 125-page A4 Word Document manuscript will result in a paperback book of approximately 260 pages once pasted into the KDP standard 5" × 8" paperback template. The template reads like a book with the correct margins on each side of the page.

Have a look at non-fiction books on your bookshelf to see how to lay out the first few pages; title page, copyright, dedication, contents, and so on. You are aiming for your template manuscript to present just how you want your finished book to look. Make sure you have all the pages, including blank pages, correctly set and numbered, and that they match with the contents page.

Once you have your completed, fully-edited and formatted manuscript, you are now ready to go on to upload your file. Your book cover PDF can be uploaded later.

Uploading files to a digital platform can be daunting if this is your first time. That is perfectly natural, and not unsurprising, but don't let fear of technology stop you at this point. Many creative people, and that includes writers, find navigating the internet and translating technological language, frightening and off-putting. There are many online companies that will take full advantage of this fear, and will happily relieve you of your hard-earned money simply for doing what you can do yourself on your own computer or laptop. Take your time, keep a back-up of your manuscript and cover design on a memory stick just in case the absolute worst thing happens.

Whatever your ethical thoughts on Amazon, they are one of the largest book internet platforms in the world, and their reach is mind blowing. In terms of people being able to find your book online, everybody has heard of Amazon and the platform is easy to use. Do look at other platforms for comparisons on what each can offer you, but don't overthink it at this stage. You will learn through experience which ones might give you added reach across the market and are suitable for you.

KDP is the publishing platform for Kindle and Amazon Books. Other platforms use similar processes for uploading manuscript files.

Here is a brief guide for uploading onto KDP:

- Firstly, you will need to sign up and create an account with a username and password.
- Fill in all the details for your book. Use your back-of-book blurb as a guide for the description, but make it even shorter and snappier.
- Choose seven words or short phrases, not included in the title, that people searching for a book like yours might use.
- Select two browser categories; for example: non-fiction/social, science/gay studies, and non-fiction/mind, body and spirit.

- You are then asked if your book contains adult content. If you tick the box it means it is unsuitable for those under the age of eighteen. However, 'adult content' is a term that is plainly very vague and forces the author to self-censor their work and means that others will make arbitrary decisions without knowing exactly what the 'adult content' is. It basically means that if someone buys your book from an online platform and then complains that it was not properly labelled as containing 'adult content', the platform can lay the blame with the author as this question is part of their setting-up process. It is about liability. Having a vague descriptive like 'adult content' ensures that any complaint is covered. To allay any concerns you may have, without disadvantaging your online presence, you could add a warning to the back of your book stating that it contains sexual content or references that may upset some readers.
- Next you are asked whether you want to use a free assigned ISBN. You can use your own ISBN purchased from Nielson Book UK which will give you the option to sell your book across multiple platforms; i.e. Barnes & Noble, IngramSpark, Smashwords, etc. Every book must have an ISBN.
- Then choose your print options: how you want your book to be printed, i.e. black and white interior with white paper, trim size 5″ × 8″ (standard paperback size), and no bleed, i.e. all the pages fit within the page margins; and the cover finish either glossy or matt.
- Upload your manuscript and cover as separate PDFs.

Once all this is done, you can use the KDP Preview Launcher to see what your book will look like. Look through this thoroughly, page by page, to make sure there are no glitches. You can always go back, do the amendments, and re-upload your manuscript as many times as you need to if there are things that need to be changed. Double-check that the page numbering is correct and matches your contents page, as extra blank pages are sometimes added at the front and back in the uploading process.

If you are happy with everything, you can now approve, and order a proof copy. A proof copy is essential, even if you think everything looks okay on the screen, it is not always the case when you have the physical book in your hands. The cover might be misaligned or the quality of the finish not as you expected. This will take a week or so to arrive and there is a cost for the print and delivery, but it is worth it for your peace of mind.

Once you have received your proof copy and you are happy with how everything looks, then is the time to think about your launch and put your marketing plans into action.

15. Telling *their* Story: JD Glass

JD Glass was born in New York City and now lives in Chicago. 'Proudly based in GenX', she is a gay woman who identifies as lesbian, 'a word that is so hard for everyone to use, so I try to reclaim it,' she says.

It's funny when I think on it, I've been writing stories ever since I could tell them, with my first written story in kindergarten, titled *A Mouse in the House*. Now granted, my family lived in an apartment at the time, but honestly, I didn't quite know the difference between a house, a home, or an apartment. To me, anywhere you lived was a house, a home, an apartment, they were all the same, so long as it was yours.

But putting my misunderstanding of nomenclature aside, what no one knew then, not even me, that this was the beginning of my telling stories that would reflect or more accurately mirror my own life events and locations.

My coming out process was difficult: I was raised to know that lying was wrong, perhaps one of the biggest sins a person could commit, outside of murder, rape, or theft, and being a truthful person from the outset, as I began to realise that I in fact wasn't straight at all, I found myself in direct turmoil. 'Gay' was a sin according to the Catholic Church, the same church that had posters up on the walls of the rec centre that, in its attempt to educate about abortion, told how an embryo developed into a foetus, and things like a penchant for art, preference for the colour red, and attraction to dark hair would arise and then it ended with, 'on the 40th day' or some such timeline like that, 'my mother killed me.'

This heavy-handed abortion message aside, I couldn't understand one thing: if the Church was using the science of development, as they understood it, to declare that this little tadpole with limbs and a tail already liked Thai food, the colour red, and dark-haired suitors, then how in the world didn't it also make sense that if someone was gay, it was part of all that? Thai food and red, artistic leanings and dark hair, all determined before the tail had even completely disappeared.

Yet, this thing, this being gay, which I already knew was as immutable as my own eye colour, an aspect of self that the Church itself, using its own logic, weirdly acknowledged, was something I was born with – it was a sin.

Somehow, knowing that this was a thing that was as natural as my favourite colour, my favourite food, even favourite scent (according to the posters), meant that I was made that way, and I knew that no matter what, in the very end of things, lying would be the worst thing I could do; it would strip me of my authenticity, of my own sense of right and wrong, the ability to discern the truth from lies, because I myself, would be a liar.

I found myself nauseated when the topic came up, the physical tearing in my stomach a direct reflection of the tearing in my sense of self. When I finally made my own peace with it, I knew I would tell my parents. I didn't know how, and I didn't know when, but I knew that I would, and I assumed this, they were my parents, I was their daughter – they loved me. They always told us (I have two younger siblings) that we could tell them anything. We would be okay. We'd figure it out.

And somehow, in the weird way that life works, that very night, the night of the first day I'd been able to say to myself I was gay, the night of the day I'd promised myself I would find the right time and tell my parents...

They called me to their room to talk.

Someone had outed me.

And my relief at their knowing turned in an instant, to pain. Actual physical pain because they beat me bloody and tried to force me to say that I wasn't gay, or bi, or anything like that at all.

This was the beginning of a few years of true torture, physically and psychologically, and the only thing that kept me going was the internal knowledge that I was ethically right, and after a while, the friends I had, not only knew, but loved me exactly as I was.

There's the thing – I survived.

There had been times that were painful, and times that were crushingly lonely. But the strength of being able to not only know myself, but to own myself, got me through, even though I would never have thought I could.

The protests I could occasionally catch sight of on the evening news, the headlines of activists in the fights against homophobia in its various active incarnations, and the occasional glimpse of a person or character in a tv show or a comic book…these things helped me and got me through, even before I found more friends and eventually, the community.

One day I realised that in a world of several billion people, there was no way I could be the only one who'd experienced this sort of thing, and that maybe, somewhere, there was a young person who felt alone, who was isolated, who was wondering if they could hold on, survive, get to tomorrow. And so I wrote. And kept writing.

Finally, my first book came out and since then, I get emails from people of all ages that thank me for writing our story, for giving them hope, and for some, yes, saving their life. So, I keep writing.

Punk Like Me by J D Glass and other books by the author are available on Amazon. J D Glass can be found on Twitter @JD Glass Instagram @jdglass_story_artist/ and Facebook @jdglass2

Part Three: Marketing

Throughout the writing process, and especially now that everything you can do to improve your manuscript, the design of your book cover, and the engagement you've had with interviewees, your editor, and other professionals you've turned to for help and advice, has all been done, there comes an inevitable lull. Doubts start to set in. Am I on the right track? Will people understand what I've tried to do with my book? Will my LGBTQ+ community get it? Is it any good? Is it a waste of time? Who am I kidding?

All these thoughts and emotions are perfectly normal for all writers, and these feelings occur at different stages of the writing journey. It is the case, no matter what level of publishing you are at. Do not panic.

When you get those doubting voices in your head, just think about what you've achieved so far.

You are further down the road than you were this time last year, last month, or even last week. Don't give up. If you need a short break from things just to get away from it all for a while, then do so. Don't be hard on yourself. The world will not tip over if you leave the computer screen and social media for a while, and you will come back refreshed and raring to go again. Self-publishing means that you are in charge of when things get done.

In this section we are going to talk about marketing, helping your book to sell and your message to get heard.

Once you are ready, the enjoyment of finally being able to talk about your book as a real thing, can begin.

16. Make A Plan

After publishing your book, you might then experience an intense feeling of having to let your baby go, and that can be difficult. The project you have loved and poured your heart and soul into for the past couple of years, or more, has finally come to fruition, but then what? You want the best response your book can get and getting it out to your audience will not happen without some work and involvement from you. You can do this most effectively by being the best parent you can be to your baby by giving it a gentle guiding hand, rather than being the pushy loud parent no one likes.

To get your book noticed you will have to do a lot of stuff and this is called *marketing*, putting you and your book, in front of as many potential customers as you can.

Marketing and promoting can be a slog, and at first it can feel extremely frustrating, as if you're getting nowhere fast, despite all your efforts. It can also be hugely rewarding in so many ways, not least of all are the fascinating people you will get to meet, many of whom will become your allies.

If the idea of marketing you and your book is something you are not comfortable with, don't worry, you are not alone in this. Afterall, it is the antithesis of writing. Where before you spent hours each day locked away deep in the writing process, to market your book you will now need to find and connect with other people to create a buzz around you. For some this is daunting, and it doesn't come naturally, even for famous bestselling authors. Take heart because there is a lot you can do even if you're not the most confident of people. You will also find that by reaching out to others and talking about your book and your story that they will admire you and your tenacity for just getting the job of writing your book done in the first place.

Tracking down your LGBTQ+ tribe and people who will naturally have an interest in what your book is about will also reward you with many fruitful connections and other contacts that will bear unexpected links and interactions later on.

Don't feel that you have to do everything mentioned in this and the following chapters on marketing straight away. Instead, take what feels right for you and adapt other things that could be useful.

What exactly is marketing?

It is 'the business process of creating relationships with, and satisfying, customers.' This is the standard definition, and it is as simple as that.

The idea of yelling about how brilliant your book is, and what an excellent job you've done in writing and producing it, is excruciatingly difficult for many, and you might see any such self-promotion as showing-off and ungracious.

For LGBTQ+ people especially, we are more aware than most of drawing unwanted attention, or even positive praise, our way. Often, we don't believe it when people say nice things to us or about us, and our instinct is to look for the hidden messages of prejudice, the slightest intonation of scorn, or the tell of unfriendly body language.

Blowing our own trumpet is something most of us are simply not used to.

To help you 'let go' of your book, try to think of it as an exciting new product you've discovered that you need to tell other people about. Step back a bit and try to distance yourself and your personal attachment to it. Try to see it as others do who have lived those experiences you write about. How might they view your book? Probably as the fulfilment of something they have been waiting all their lives to find and finally have the answers they have longed for.

By not telling people about your book, you will be doing them a disservice.

When it comes to your book launch and its continual promotion afterwards, to help organise things, create a spreadsheet, either on paper or on the computer, and do this as soon as you have ordered your proof copy.

Start with your key launch date. Is that going to coincide with a special LGBTQ+ event on the calendar? Whatever the date is, work in both directions, back-and-forth, from there.

Once your proof copy arrives, and you are happy with it, you will need to allow a couple more weeks for your author copies to be delivered. These are the copies you will need for reviews, events, a launch party, competitions, and any free handouts.

Make a list of all the podcasts, radio shows, and blogs you would like to get invited on to and start contacting them. Use MatchMaker FM to approach podcasters appropriate to your LGBTQ+ topic. Perhaps there are magazines you could write articles for or organisations you could talk to about being on a panel discussion or who might be interested in your book. Send them a press release (see sub-chapter: 16.6 Write A Press Release). As you get confirmation back from each of your enquiries, whether they say they would love to have you on or share something from you on their blog, schedule all this information onto your spreadsheet, plus the time you will need to write any articles or provide complementary copies of your book.

At this drawing-up of plans stage, you might also consider making an *author business plan*, or even just write down your dream of where you want to be in one, two to three, and five-years' time. If you've little intention of doing anything beyond this book, that's fine, but it will still help to think about where you aim to be with it in a year or two.

Here are some things to think about when planning your marketing strategy:

- Who is your typical customer and where can you find them? (See sub-chapter: 16.4 Defining Your Typical Customer). Once you know this important piece of information, you can think about what you need to do to reach them.
- Which social media platforms are you going to use, and what kind of posts are you going to put up? (see chapter: 23. Social Media).
- Marketing material: will you need business cards for events, leaflets to distribute to shops and at markets, posters for a book launch and panel discussions, and possibly a website designed?
- Create contact lists: journalists, bloggers, podcasters, organisations, book clubs, charities, influencers, and anyone else who might help, and in what way. Check through your follower lists on social media. Use Google to find connections.

Log as much information as you can onto your spreadsheet with dates, costs you incur, and outcomes as you progress. Keep it updated and relevant. If something doesn't work, make a note of the reasons why and learn as you go.

It can be helpful to have a brand file on your computer, so that you can instantly access your photo headshots, logo, book cover, author bio etc., if someone asks for any of these things. Also, start a file of pictures you can use across social media. Social media is pretty free when it comes to copyright, but if you use an image that belongs to someone else be prepared for them to ask you to remove it. This is unlikely to happen unless you have a huge following, or are an 'influencer'. If you are in that category, everything you post will be scrutinised.

With a concise plan you will be able to control how much marketing you do. You will discover what works for you and your book, and not feel overawed and pressured into doing anything you are not entirely comfortable with.

16.1 Get Leverage In Your Community

Getting leverage, and influence, in your community means doing this both in the area you live, and importantly, within your LGBTQ+ community. Make as many people as possible aware of you and your book, and the message you are trying to spread. Being a big fish in a small pond will give you masses of confidence and kudos for when you dip your toe into the bigger, wider waters.

Collaborate. Reach out to LGBTQ+ organisations such as Stonewall UK, LGBT Switchboard, Mindout, and many more you can find online (there is a list of some helpful links at the back of this book). Seek out other LGBTQ+ writers, podcasts, and bloggers. Look for groups on MeetUp.com. While many big cities have vibrant LGBTQ+ communities, it is not the same across all parts of the country. To build your network you will need to look for like-minded people. Gays, lesbians, bi, trans, or whoever your tribe are, they are out there, you just need to be a little bold and make the first move. Introduce yourself, tell them about your book and how you hope it will help others in the same situation. You'll be surprised at the interest you'll get back.

Once you find these people, form partnerships and alliances, and keep them close. What can you do for each other? Can they introduce you to other people they know who might also be interested in what you have written about? Build on all your relationships.

It is sometimes said that 'so-and-so' only got where they did because of who they knew. This reveals some truth, but it does not take into account all the hard work that goes into nurturing relationships with, for instance, bookshop owners, bloggers, other writers, and people from all walks of life interested in the same LGBTQ+ issues as you. Making and cultivating these connections and relationships is vital. They can all lead to doors being opened that you may never have thought of before.

What you must avoid is launching your book into a silent vacuum. This doesn't mean that you need to hound people, but just keep you and your book on people's radar. Promote yourself, not as the author of just this one book, but as a 'writer' to as wide an audience as possible.

16.2 Writing Competitions

You might consider entering writing competitions. If you win or get short-listed it can be a valuable asset to your marketing. Cambridge based Encompass Network run LGBTQ+ creative writing competitions, as does Outstanding Stories. The LAMBDA Literary Awards, also known as 'the Lammys', also hold literature festivals, and writers' retreats, for all LGBTQ+ literary genres. Another excellent competition, open to non-published first-time LGBTQ+ titles, is the Polari Prize.

There are many other competitions that are not specifically LGBTQ+, which you can also enter. All competitions have various submission rules and some charge a fee for entry. They run at different times of the year, internationally and nationally. Most competitions require that you enter a new book, one published within the last year, so entering one or two carefully researched competitions might be something to include in your marketing plan.

16.3 The Email Mailing List

One method to promote your book is to build a huge mailing list of people who have at least an inkling of interest in the subject matter. A list comprising 10,000 email addresses seems to be the charmed goal.

However, there are a few points to consider:

Mailchimp, the popular platform that provides distribution of flyers, newsletters, and emails to people, start charging a fee for subscriber lists with over 2,000 email addresses. Secondly, the 2018 introduction of the EU's GDPR (General Data Protection Regulation), which still applies in the UK since leaving the EU, stipulates that you cannot send unsolicited material by email, or keep people's details on record, unless they specifically ask you to. In other words, they have to subscribe to be on your email list.

Once you have your extensive email list, the object then is to sell your book to them directly by offering special deals, freebies, and extras to hook them in. You can also encourage a clique from your list to become your next book beta readers, perhaps naming them the 'Elite', 'Prime Team', 'Gold' or 'VIP Members'. These people, your fans, will then review your books. Given the push and incentive to do so, they'll also create interest around a new cover reveal, and generally act as your PR, not only in the launch weeks but into the future. The larger cohort of your email subscribers can be called to action through setting competitions, inviting them to book signings, and anything else you can come up with to keep their interest.

But how do you go about building a mailing list of 10,000 individuals?

The principle is relatively simple and it goes like this:

In the back of your e-book you place a link to a sign-up page on your website, this is where having a website is essential. There you offer prospective subscribers something for free. This could be a free chapter or two from your next book, or a book from your back catalogue. In return for the freebie, you obtain their email address. From your subscriber's perspective, they are getting something for free and have signed up to your newsletter which is of interest to them. This could be about what you are up to and include content around LGBTQ+ issues. Your primary goal is to build a relationship with them and boost loyalty to your brand.

The simplicity of this idea is its appeal. It doesn't cost you anything to get started, only indirectly in that you need to give something away as a hook-in, and it runs itself (check Mailchimp's website for up-to-date terms and conditions).

To build the email list and for it to work well, with thousands of subscribers who want to hear about your books and the latest news from you, there are some essential things you require:

Firstly, you need at least three books, although the consensus seems to be erring towards five. E-book number one should be permanently available as a free enticer (you will need to confirm if this is possible with your digital platform). Links that send the reader through to your website subscriber page should be at the front and back of this perma-free e-book. Many people who download free e-books don't even bother to read them, so having the link only positioned at the back of the book is not enough. Having this book permanently free will ensure some downloads, but you will still need to market it and push it to get onto any of the ranking lists. It will still not 'sell' itself even as a give-away. You will need to be shrewd with the categories you put your book into. This is known as metadata. The principle is to narrow your category group down as far as you can, so that anyone searching for an LGBTQ+ book on your topic will be able to find it.

Once they have signed up by giving you their email address, they are then led to the next stage to entice them into purchasing your second book, which you offer at a reduced price they cannot get anywhere else. It is your third or latest book that is the one you really want to sell them through your newsletter, and hopefully by then you will have generated enough interest to hook people in.

The mailing list is a tool that, once it has grown in size, can be an effective and useful means of marketing, but don't expect it to grow overnight. Only once you have near the magic number of 10,000 email addresses will it start to generate the momentum you need for it to work well. That is not to say that starting small and growing your list organically is not something you might consider doing as part of your marketing strategy.

16.4 Defining Your Typical Customer

The biggest question you need to ask, is who might your customers be?

Not everyone who reads, or who is LGBTQ+, will be interested in buying a book on the subject. You will need to discover exactly the type of person your core customer is, so that any marketing or promotions you do can be tailored towards them to grab their attention and interest.

A good place to start is to consider the problem your book solves, and the needs it fulfils. Think of it this way: a fence is a boundary between two gardens. That is the fundamental problem it solves in marking out the boundary.

But the needs a fence fulfils might include creating privacy, blocking out noise, security, keeping children, and pets, safe or obscuring unsightly views. The individual needs your book answers might be many things. It will undoubtedly solve a fundamental problem of a lack of information for people in the same situation. The needs it fulfils might also include affirming for the reader that they are not alone, how relationships with others might be affected and/or resolved, answering fundamental questions about homosexuality, and much, much more. For LGBTQ+ people, all or some of these, and other identifiable needs, might be what draws them to your book.

Being able to identify these needs means that you can target those niche sectors of the market.

This is not an easy task, and it will take some time, but the effort will be worth it. Even if you think that your readers are likely to be just like you, start by writing a list of what you think their demographic characteristics are most likely to be: what gender they identify as; how they view their sexuality. Are they aged between sixteen and eighteen, or thirty-five to fifty, or older? Do they do 'outdoorsy' activities, listen to a certain style of music, or watch costume dramas on TV? Where do they go for their social media? Is Facebook where you're going to find them (see chapter: 23. Social Media), possibly not if they're typically under thirty.

Here are some ideas to help build a picture of your typical customer:

- Go to Amazon and look for books that are similar to yours. Look at the people who leave reviews; try to identify the type of person reading those books.

- What do their reviews say about them? Look at the 'also bought' recommendations at the bottom.
- Look for groups on Facebook that would have a natural interest in your subject. What is the demographic makeup of such groups?
- Search online for other groups and organisations you think would naturally fit well with your subject; again, who are these people?

Try to be as specific as you can in visualising the primary purchaser of your book. The more you can find out about them, the better, and the easier it will be to 'speak' to them and connect with them. From this information build up a stock of relevant images in a social media picture library, that you know your core audience will instantly relate to.

16.5 Create An Elevator Pitch

This might sound a bit over-the-top and not something you think necessary, but essentially an elevator pitch means having the words ready and easy to recall whenever someone asks you what your book is about and why you wrote it. Scrabbling around for something pithy and intelligent to say on the spur of the moment is never going to work well. What you want, is to be able to reply with seamless effort and confidence, that makes your book sound interesting and irresistible.

Think of an elevator pitch as just that. Something short and succinct that will ignite someone's interest, and which can be said out loud in the time it takes to go a couple of floors up in a lift or elevator, about 20 seconds.

Here are some tips:

- Write down the essence of what your book is about in no more than 50 words.
- What is/are the key thing/s someone will learn from reading your book?
- Add-in your unique selling point; your USP. This will often be your own story, and why you wrote your book.
- Put your topic into a context that everyone will understand. For instance, 'If you're ready to come out, my book will help with what to say, and when, to friends, family and work colleagues.'

Take all the points above and make them into a sentence which is no more than 50 words in length. Then think of a snappy tagline. As an example, 'Why, against all odds, do homosexuals exist?', was the tagline I used for my book *This Forbidden Fruit*. Add your tagline to the end of your fifty-word pitch. Now edit that down to keep it within the short and punchy fifty-word limit.

Read it out loud. You could even record yourself saying it, then play it back so that you can hear how it sounds. Change the words around, reshape it, and replace words you are not comfortable saying with the kind of language you would use daily. You don't want your pitch to sound like a hard sell, you want it to be natural, warm and sincere.

Keep going over your pitch saying it out loud, in the car, the shower, all the time, until it trips off the tongue without you having to think about it. Test it out on friends and family. The more times you say these few words to people, the easier it will become, but make sure that each time you say it, it sounds like it is the first time. People don't want to feel you're just repeating a script, or that you're trying to sell your book to them – though of course, that is the objective. You want people to say, 'That sounds really interesting', and mean it. If they say, 'Tell me more', you can add a short anecdote.

Think in terms of what it would be like to be interviewed on a live radio show, where you've only got a limited amount of time to get your message across. You cannot afford to ramble. Above all, you want to establish a rapport, especially with strangers, so give them a chance to tell you their related experience. Then you can point them towards your social media or website, with a business card if you have one, or tell them where they can find links to purchase your book. Better still, tell them where they can buy a copy from an independent bookshop, and to let the owner know that you sent them along.

16.6 Write A Press Release

Before the days of the internet, when news stories could only be read in newspapers, magazines, or were aired on radio and television to strict timetables, journalists, and editors had a finite amount of copy and airtime to fill. Each month they would be sent press releases from people wanting their story to be featured, and they had to choose what did and did not get used. There was, in those days, a much smaller pool of writers vying for their attention, and creating copy was seen as the profession of a very few people who were viewed as being somewhere on the spectrum between a seedy hack and a well-respected broadsheet investigative journalist, with the odd magazine features writer somewhere in the middle.

Today, with the almost unlimited number of opportunities provided by the internet to get your work out there, and on a rolling twenty-four-hour schedule; bloggers, journalists, and editors alike are constantly on the lookout for interesting stories, especially ones that are written for them. LGBTQ+ stories are always hot news, but they still need to be pushed. If you're able to package your story into a format which immediately grabs the journalist's, blogger's, or editor's attention, you're almost certain to get a positive response. Don't send out a generic press release to the whole world though, make it personal and ensure it gets to the right person.

A press release is a short, preferably, one or two page document that explains what your book is about and why you wrote it. It is important that it is engaging and hooks people's interest immediately.

Here are a few things that will *definitely* get you noticed:

- A shocking, captivating, unique personal story: 'I literally lost my feet, including my favourite ruby slippers, in a storm, and had them surgically re-attached, slippers and all!'
- A unique, fascinating, yet topical book subject. *Topical* is the crucial word here. If when you're writing your story, you sense a shift in public awareness towards your particular sector of the LGBTQ+ community, get it written and out there. Interest will wane quickly and soon be yesterday's news.
- A rare or prestigious book award (think Booker Prize or Women's Book Award). If you have one of these, people will be contacting you anyway.
- An achievement that is really impressive: 'I was the first openly gay astronaut'.
- Celebrity endorsement. Not just a B-lister, but a genuine household name, who can and is willing to support you and your story with their own.
- Get on the bandwagon of the hottest topic of the moment, for instance climate change, politics, or war. Something that everybody is talking about. Slightly different to 'unique, fascinating and

topical' which implies something rarer that peaks in interest.

Write your press release in the third person as if it is from an agent or PR company. The points above will get you and your book noticed, but if you do not fit these particular remits it does not mean that you cannot gain some interest.

Your advantage is that people are genuinely interested in the human story, and that your LGBTQ+ story is unique.

Here is a press release standard layout:

- At the top of your press release in bold you should write 'For Immediate Release' or 'New Book Press Release'. This tells the person receiving it that it is something they need to look at or pass on to the relevant person right away.
- Next, a fantastic hook as your headline. Think how your book might appear as a headline in a newspaper. Short, snappy, and eye-catching. 'True-life stories of divorced gay men who have children', was the headline used for the press release for my book *Gay Dad*.
- An image of the book cover. Next to that the title, author name, and publication date and, if you can, 'perfect timing for …' something relevant such as Father's Day, Pride season, National Coming Out Day, etc.
- Next, comes the sub-headline (no longer than a sentence). For example, 'Emotionally charged, here are the true-life stories of ten homosexual men who married women and had children before coming out.'

- Then a thought-provoking quote from the book to get the reader's attention. 'I will never forget the image of me leaving my wife and two babies on the doorstep, as I walked away with a bin bag of clothes to the car. My father didn't talk to me for two years.'
- The book's vital information: ISBN, the format your book can be bought in, i.e. hardback, paperback, e-book, or audiobook. Number of pages, RRP, published by, and links to your website and social media.
- The body of the press release should be just as attention grabbing. You can do this by posing a question as a hook: 'How many gay men end up marrying women?' Give a clear and concise answer and use your back-of-book blurb as a starting point, but don't copy it word-for-word.
- If you have a foreword written by a celebrity, mention it and quote from it (similarly, don't put the whole foreword into your press release, just a pertinent quote). You can also use any review quotes you have, but only if they're substantial, i.e. from well-known sources. Only say you've got 30 reviews on Amazon if that is true, because it will be checked.
- An image of you, the author (if you can), plus an important quote from you about the book. Avoid sounding dull. Think, 'This book changed my life …' or 'I came out writing this book …'
- Add your contact details (email, phone), whether you are happy to take interviews and stipulate if you will consider press, radio, or TV. Make it clear whether your image can be used or not.
- Confirm that you are happy to supply review copies on request.

All this should appear on the first page. If you really can't fit the crux of what your book is about onto one page, go onto a second, but make sure you are not overdressing or repeating something you've already stated. Highlight the interest your book will have for groups, organisations, and LGBTQ+ communities and give suggestions for features and articles in the form of thought-provoking questions:

'Can a gay man really fall in love with a woman, doesn't that mean he's bisexual?'

'Should there be more discussion in schools about different family set-ups and lifestyles?'

'Now that we have same-sex marriage in the UK, is there anything left for the gay community to achieve?'

Add your author-bio on the second page. Make it impactful and gripping, not a retelling of the book. Include any relevant groups or organisations you belong to, and any applicable, and meaningful, achievements you may have. If there is space, add something about yourself that won't be found in the book. For instance, how you can often be found wild-water swimming or that you have a large collection of Cuban cigars.

End the press release with three hashtag symbols centred at the bottom of the page.

Remember: A book being released is not news, so you must make your LGBTQ+ story newsworthy. A well-crafted press release will help you do that.

How do you get your press release out to journalists and bloggers? As with anything, you can pay someone to do this for you, but I would be wary of paying a syndication service to do a mass hit, as such distributed promotional emails are very often blocked by inbox settings and never reach the intended agencies or professionals. A lot of exposure does not necessarily transpose into actual interest. You could use a PR company and give them the responsibility. They will compose a press release as part of the service they will provide and charge you for.

I used a PR company for promoting *Gay Dad*. Whether it was worth the cost in terms of immediate book sales, is difficult to quantify, but in terms of building my platform, brand, and reputation through the promotional opportunities I was given, it undoubtedly was.

If you do not want to hire a PR company or use a syndication service, the answer to how to reach the journalists, bloggers, and editors you want to, is to gather the information yourself, which is perfectly feasible although more work for you.

If you can, send your press release out in advance of your book launch date, but it is not essential; in fact, having some reviews and back-up information about how well your book is being received can be an advantage to garnering more interest. Write a personal email, with your press release attached, to the different journalists, bloggers, and editors on various dates dependent on what they might be able to offer you. On your spreadsheet, note the date you send the email to them and what their response is; whether they require a review copy, would like to set up an interview, or get you on their podcast.

This will all take time, especially if they request a copy of your book, so plan everything carefully. It's easy, in the rush of so much activity, to overlook an email that might have turned out to be a door-opener. Make sure that you follow-up all enquiries and correspondence, even if they have declined or you wish to decline them.

17. Telling *their* Story: Frederic Davies

Frederic Davies is the author of *Fathers and Sons*, a book about his coming out story, and how he rebuilt his life as a gay man after being married to a woman and having two children together. It is a story that depicts the pain of family breakdown and its traumatic aftermath.

I asked Frederic why he felt compelled to write and publish his story?

There were actually two reasons why I felt I had to. I had a friend who came out a few years before I did and, just like me, he had been married and had children. That gave me the confidence and reassurance I needed, knowing that my friend had walked the same path before me, and that I wasn't the only married man in the world who felt like this.

Interestingly, when my friend read my book, he was surprised to find that I'd written about the key role he had in my coming out story. He was oblivious to the importance he played in my life and he completely underestimated what he had done for me. Not everyone has a friend like this. I wanted my book to provide the support for other gay dads who feel lost, alone and isolated.

The second reason is that I wanted to take this opportunity to tell my children, who were eight and eleven years old at the time, about what was going on in my head when I left. Why I felt I had no choice, and to try to put my side of the story so that they have all the facts concerning my actions. I am not looking for their approval, rather that they understand what was going on for me at the time. I've tried to talk to them about this period in my life, but the conversations have been awkward. I hope that a written account is a better way to reach out to them.

My son, who is now 31, is still, after 20 years, very angry with me. I hope that by explaining that I was on the verge of a mental breakdown and felt that I had no choice, it will help repair some of his unresolved issues, and will lead to an improved relationship.

What were your expectations of the process of writing your book to the reality of publishing it?

Having never written a book before, I totally underestimated the size of the task. I wasn't writing constantly, but the project took me more than two years to complete, and my original estimate was a maximum of one year.

I soon realised that my priority was to get the words onto the page, so I wasn't concerned about paragraphs, punctuation, or layout, more just letting the story flow from my memory to my typing fingers. I knew the aesthetics could be sorted out later. I also knew there were going to be emotional parts of my story that I would need to revisit, but it wasn't until I started that I realised, to be able to write an account in such detail, I had to go back in time and relive the event. This meant feeling the painful emotions just as I had done the first time. It was the only way I would be able to share every thought, fact, and emotion with the reader. As a result, I could only write in periods of two to three hours, as I found the task emotionally draining and exhausting and, sometimes, I would need to take a nap afterwards to recover.

I guess that although I knew I was going to tell my story, and this would involve very personal details, I wasn't prepared for how much of myself I would need to put into the book. I also had to enlist the help of an executive coach and counsellor to help me dig into some of the painful memories, as I'd locked them away, and I struggled to revisit them.

For example, the events of the day I left my wife were so painful that I couldn't write that chapter until the rest of the book was complete. Then I went back and did it. There were times when I wasn't sure if this chapter would get written at all, as the memories were still so painful, even after 20 years.

I thought I had remembered my entire coming out story, and all of the individual events that had taken place, but when I came to write them down there were many small details that I'd either forgotten about, or blocked out, and they only came back to me when I allowed my mind to open and travel back into the past.

Did you think about what the consequences of telling your story so publicly might be?

Yes, I did. And I am happy to accept those consequences, whatever they are. I feel that it is my duty to tell my story, to help others in a similar situation who come after me. When I made the decision to come out as gay, I knew there was going to be a huge impact on my family, and telling my story feels like a continuation of that journey. I've had to face challenges many times in the past in order to be my true and authentic self and I am certainly not prepared to be anything less than one hundred percent honest now, otherwise I would feel that I am betraying myself.

What has the reaction of your family been to the book?

My family is quite small, so I only have a few family members to share my book with. My brother has been very supportive and, surprisingly, there were many aspects of my story that he was unaware of, even though we grew up together in the same house. As a result of discussing some of our childhood events, as I gathered information for my book, he told me how he had defended me at school when his friends called me gay. I was completely shocked when I found this out. Firstly, I couldn't believe my brother hadn't told me this before, and secondly, that even at that young age, other people could see evidence of my sexuality that I was oblivious to. One positive outcome is that our honesty has brought my brother and I much closer together.

My daughter, now 28, has concerns about reading the book as she's worried that it will open up old wounds and that, like me, she will have to revisit emotionally difficult things from the past she has buried. My hope is that in time she will overcome these feelings and that curiosity will get the better of her.

Unfortunately, the relationship with my ex-wife continues to be very difficult. For the first ten years after we split-up we had little or no contact as she was so angry and couldn't forgive me for what I had done to her and the devastation I had inflicted on our family. Then, for a time, there seemed to be some improvement in our relationship. We met up and had dinner a couple of times and we were able to talk about some of the good times in our marriage and share happy memories of the children growing up but unfortunately this was short lived. Several years ago, my ex-wife remarried, and I hoped that this would be a turning point, but sadly it was not. Our relationship hasn't improved, and actually it has got worse, with no contact for many months. My hope is that my book will provide her with an alternative view of our story and an explanation of my thoughts and actions, provide some answers, and hopefully closure. My belief, however, is that the hurt and anger are still so raw, that even after 20 years, it would be too painful for her to read.

Has your son read it? Has he made contact?

No, my son has not made contact, and, to my knowledge, he hasn't read it. I have asked my daughter to share it with him, as I think she is the only person he will listen to regarding his relationship with me. My hope is that even if he resists initially, over time he will be curious, and take a look. To add to my sadness, my son and his wife had another baby recently, so I am now a grandad for the second time, but with no access to either of my grandsons.

What about your wider family and friends, what has their reaction been?

I've received very positive reactions so far. I've had a lot of great feedback from friends, both gay and straight. Many of my gay friends said that they were surprised in the similarities between their childhood emotions and mine, that they too had an overwhelming feeling of being different as they grew up, but not understanding why. Many people have commented on my bravery at making such a difficult, life-changing decision, but I really didn't see it like that at the time. It just felt like something that was unavoidable in the end. Now, when I look back, I can see that it did take courage and I want others to be inspired to do the same.

Did you tell your family that you were going to write your book beforehand?

I told my daughter when the book was almost complete, and initially she was shocked that I had decided to tell the world my story. This was not the reaction I had expected. She asked if she could read it before publication, but I refused as I didn't want to get into a discussion or argument about whether a fact or element of the story was correct or not. I was clear that this book was *my* version of the events that took place, and I understand that my daughter may have different recollections, but I wasn't prepared to negotiate. My daughter also asked me to use a penname as she didn't want the book to be directly associated with her. I would have been happy to use my real name, but I certainly didn't want to cause my daughter any further upset or anguish, and I did not want to run the risk of damaging our relationship, so I was happy to agree to that.

How do you feel now, after writing your book, and having it published?

To be honest, I am still in a state of shock. Having talked about my book for so long, and when people asked how the writing was going, I would say, 'just fine', and that 'it should be finished in a couple of months'. Then the launch day arrived. I am now a published author and it feels a bit surreal.

It's a great feeling to know that my personal story is out in the world for other people to read, and my hope is that it gives them some strength and confidence to live their lives authentically. Through the process of writing, I realised I was still carrying an enormous amount of guilt for the devastation I caused my family and particularly my children. I have been able to work through those feelings and discard much of that guilt, and as a result I feel that a weight has been lifted from my shoulders.

The entire process has been cathartic. I've had to face feelings, emotions, and pain, head on and to deal with them, but finally, I can move forward.

Frederic Davies' book *Fathers and Sons* is available on Amazon. Frederic can be found on Twitter @frederic_davies on Facebook @fredericdavies and on Instagram @fredericdavies2020

18. Before You Press Publish

It is worth noting that the biggest industry book launch days happen in October, ready for the Christmas market. You don't have to coincide with this date, of course, but you might tie your book launch in with another special calendar date, holiday or festival to give it the maximum coverage it can get. Pride month, World AIDS day, National Coming Out day, LGBT History Month, are all landmarks in the LGBTQ+ calendar, and there are many more.

Traditional book launch campaigns start well in advance of the actual date. Large publishing houses have huge sums of money at their disposal to pay for advertising on billboards, the sides of buses, and through targeted social media advertising. Very few of us have that sort of monetary power. That does not mean that you should not launch your book with as much celebration and pizzazz as you can, and it is still a good idea, even on a small scale, to start planning this on your spreadsheet well ahead of time.

Here is a simple launch strategy, loosely based on author-preneur Mark Dawson's formula, which can be scaled to meet your budget and your ideals. Some people are lucky to have the funds to implement an effective Facebook advertising campaign (see sub-chapter: 23.2 Facebook Advertising), or a large-scale email campaign (see sub-chapter: 16.3 The Email Mailing List), but for those new to self-publishing, what follows is a practical guide to planning your book launch.

Six Weeks Prior To Launch Day:

If you intend sending out ARC (Advanced Reader Copies) of your book to bloggers or reviewers, you need to plan this well in advance. They will require time to read and review your book and you will want their reviews to coincide with your launch, or as near as possible to it.

For the self-publishing author, the way to get hold of advanced copies is to use the proof copy facility that the likes of Amazon and IngramSpark offer.

Proof copies are automatically printed with a 'Not for Resale' band around the cover. You can also add an 'Advanced Reader Copy' label in a prominent position on the first page. Remember to remove this label and re-upload your manuscript file for the final time before you publish.

Amazon delivers proofs in small batches and to one address only. If you need more, you will have to do multiple orders and will need to take this into account when planning despatching to your recipients.

Ingramspark offer a no limit order on proof copies.

One Month Prior To Launch Day:

Before you officially publish, you can set your book to pre-order on Amazon. This means that people can order it at a discounted price with the guarantee that it will be dispatched to them the minute it is launched live on the platform. There are benefits for doing this. Pre-ordered books can receive reviews, and algorithms will search for pre-ordered books and give them a favourable boost on launch day.

You should also start to think about how you can lift the number of followers you have on your social media platforms, so that when it comes to the launch and subsequent promotion, you have more new followers to engage with.

If you have an email list, one of the things you can do to encourage engagement with your up-coming book is to send out an abridged version or a few chapters and ask for feedback. Make sure you give a cut-off date when you need this back by with any recommendations or typos they might have spotted. These people will then have a vested interest in your book's success. Even small-scale involvement with just a few willing and vocal members on social media, is worth cultivating.

Any errors your team spots should be rectified straight away on the final draft Word document. Wait until all the feedback has been received before uploading the file for the last time onto your digital publishing platform and before ordering your final proof copy. In the time it will take for the proof to arrive, start to plan your launch schedule.

Think about what social media posts you should be posting over the coming weeks. Create dialogue and conversation with as many of your followers and LGBTQ+ allies as you can. Be extra lively on social media so that people start to notice you more. Join in with any writing community hashtags like #writerslift or #promolgbtq or #writingcommunity.

Think about images that might be associated with, or are similar to, the cover of your book. Post these before you then reveal your cover teaser. A few days later you can do a full cover reveal. Spruce up your social media pages: upload new banners and author portraits. Write blogs and schedule these onto LinkedIn or have them ready to upload onto your own website blog.

Keep communicating with all your contacts and people who have influence who can open doors for you. Confirm any book signings, readings or blog appearances. Know exactly what you'll be doing and where you'll be in the days leading up to and after your launch day.

One Week Prior To Launch Day:

Now is the time to send out a newsletter to your email subscribers with all the details about your book, the release date, cover, and where they will be able to get it and in what format. You could also include an exclusive extract and a special offer on another book, if you have one. You could also add a competition with a simple, relevant question to win a signed copy. Get people to send their answer to you via your social media, including a hashtag of your book title, or through your website email address.

Though it is often quicker than this, bear in mind, when announcing your launch date, that Amazon suggests allowing up to 72 hours for processing to happen before your book becomes live on their platform.

On Launch Day:

Start your blog tour (see sub-chapter: 18.4 Virtual Blog Tours). You might also hold a launch party (see sub-chapter: 18.1 Tips For Holding A Launch Party). Amazon will notify you by email to confirm that your book is available in the online store. Check this. Copy the link and post it everywhere you can online, including any Facebook and MeetUp groups you belong to, but check their rules first as some groups do not allow self-promotion. Email other relevant organisations you have a connection with.

Order your author paperback copies.

18.1 Tips For Holding A Launch Party

It is not essential to have a launch party for your book, and some view it as an expense they can do without. There is also nothing to say that you cannot have launch parties in different cities or towns over several weeks. But there are certain things you will need to incorporate in order for it to be a launch party that is successful and memorable for all the right reasons.

Here is a list of some ideas you could consider:

- Have nibbles and drinks. A glass of wine or equivalent soft drink per guest is sufficient.

- Create a guest list, and have someone on the door to check people in.
- Do not charge for entry. If there is a fee to pay on the venue, you will have to absorb that cost through book sales on the night.
- Try to get a 'relevant' LGBTQ+ celebrity to do a short introduction, and definitely if they've written a foreword in your book.
- Select appropriate music, that might be camp disco or showtunes, but be aware you cannot play music in public unless the venue is licensed to do so. You will need to check this with the venue.
- Project images or videos, (preferably your own or seek permission from the owner), in different areas of the venue (again this will be included in the venue's licence, so speak to them about what you can and cannot do). Work with them, they will have experience of these things and may have some great ideas you hadn't thought of.
- Get someone to video and photograph the event (try to get a professional who will make a good promo video). Warn your audience beforehand that there will be someone taking publicity shots or videoing and that if they do not want to be identified or filmed to let you and the photographer know.
- Send out a press release to local media, LGBTQ+ media and anyone you think might be interested.
- Have a comments book for visitors to leave messages in on their way out. Perhaps give them a free pen to write with and take away with them. Use those positive remarks in further marketing on social media.
- Give away freebies: postcards, bookmarks, balloons, or whatever is suitable. Make sure every guest goes away with a little something as a thank

you for coming. Include somewhere on the items, links to your social media, website, etc.
- Encourage people to pop their business cards and email addresses into a large bowl. Tell them that one name will be drawn out at the end of the evening for a prize, which should be something relevant to your book. State also that by entering this competition they will be entered as subscribers to your newsletter and that they can unsubscribe later if they so wish.
- Have lots of your books available to buy at a discounted price, and sit and sign them with a personal message after your talk or presentation. Take plenty of cash for a float and have a card reader for people without cash. Get someone to be responsible for taking the payments and logging the sales.
- For those leaving without purchasing a book, give them a nicely worded, encouraging order form to fill in and email back to you later. Offer a signed book at a discount and with a postcard or something free thrown in. Make sure the offer does not undercut the offer you gave other people on the night.
- Your event should be advertised with a discount incentive, such as 10% off any of your books purchased on the night, or they can purchase a copy at £5 with the event ticket (remember entry is free).
- Set up an interactive photo experience in front of a poster or relevant backdrop (think rainbows, glitter balls, or anything LGBTQ+) where people can take selfies. They will hopefully post these on their personal social media.
- Invite small businesses and relevant LGBTQ+ organisations to donate appropriate freebies to give

out as goody-bags and give them some free advertising around the event.
- At the end, tell your audience that you are happy to attend book club meetings, panel talks, go into schools, or work with other organisations, etc.
- Keep your guests entertained all the time they are there.
- The party should last no longer than an hour, maybe an hour and a half.
- Use Eventbrite or Facebook to set it up.

If the idea of standing up in front of an audience and doing a presentation about you and your book and your writing journey fills you with horror, you could ask a confident friend or drag queen to act as host for the evening. They can introduce you and you can read a few pages from your book, while leaving all the other presenting and hosting to them. Present them with some flowers at the end as a thank you.

The important thing is to engage with your audience and come across as warm and approachable.

18.2 Post-Launch

To ensure that your book sales continue to flourish, promoting and marketing cannot stop on the day the last social media promo goes out in the week after your book launches. The ongoing commitment can be overwhelming and especially so for first-time self-published authors, because much of what you need to do will be off your own back.

Why is it essential to keep promoting your book after the initial launch?

The simple answer is that as soon as you stop actively promoting your book you will see sales start to fall, and they could dry up almost completely. Promoting a book, even for bestselling authors, is an ongoing, and often laborious process. But it can and should be fun and rewarding too.

If you used Mailchimp, check your promotional email report to see who opened the email, who didn't, and who unsubscribed. For those emails that bounced back, you could include these people in a social media post if they have profiles on one of your social media platforms. Some email inboxes are set to reject emails from all sorts of unrecognised addresses and if people don't check their junk mail regularly, things can easily go unnoticed and unopened.

Engage voraciously with all your social media followers, especially those who comment, retweet, or share anything you put up.

Post any high-ranking category positions your book gets into. The category ranking can be found on your book's product page on Amazon, at the bottom in 'Product Details'. Note, rankings change all the time, so don't expect your book to remain in one position for long. Click on the category your book is in and go to the chart listing. Take screenshots and post them on your social media.

Post any good reviews you get, links to podcasts you've been on, radio interviews, blogs, etc. Keep the buzz going. Spend time connecting with any new followers. If you set a competition, don't forget to close it and announce the prize winner.

In today's instant access world, social media provides many ways of helping you to promote your book. Someone once said that self-publicity is best served by being interesting and generous and by being interested in others, and that certainly does ring true.

Try approaching other LGBTQ+ authors and ask them to give your book a review. This is called cross-promotion, whereby you promise to do the same service for them when they have a new book out. The key is to continually build and nurture relationships with relevant people.

With the evidence of five-star reviews coming in, you can now confidently approach independent bookshops to place an order with you from your stock of author copies. Take the opportunity to arrange personal in-store signings. Always be on the lookout for new and innovative ideas on how to promote and keep marketing you and your book, but also keep a look out for scams.

18.3 Merchandise

Have you thought about turning the artwork from your book cover into saleable merchandise? It can be a way to both promote your book, reinforce your branding and generate additional income. Good quality tee shirts, for instance, can make more profit per unit than a book sale.

How about using LGBTQ+ relevant quotes from your book as slogans on posters, pins and badges, mugs, flags, and tee shirts. The potential for creativity is huge.

Here is a list of things to think about to manage this successfully:

- You will need to set up a new page on your website or you can sell your promotional gifts through Zazzle, the online merchandise marketplace.
- You will need to hold a stock of items, both to sell and to have as give-aways at events.
- Consider the time this new side-line will take to set up and administer. It could be another drain on you and the cause of unnecessary stress.
- Is there already a demand for tee shirts using your book artwork? Have people made enquiries?

- Finally, the cost. Don't expect to sell loads, it will be a small, niche market, but it might be worth doing. Do the sums.

Whoever you are going to sell these products to, you will need to know your customer (see sub-chapter: 16.4 Defining Your Typical Customer). Are they young tee shirt wearers? Are they badge wearing LGBTQ+ activists or are they home workers who sit in front of the computer all day who might like a new mouse mat or quirky, logo embossed mug? Whoever they are, what you're selling must be worth them having.

Quality, unique, and eye-catching designs are what people will be drawn to, but such merchandise comes with an inflated unit cost. Always keep this in mind, work to your brand and within budget.

Giving away costly items at events might create a buzz around you and your stall, but will the outlay be too much to recoup? If you are thinking of give-aways, they should always include the book title, your author name, and your social media and website addresses somewhere on them. Limit freebies to small items such as pens, badges, or bookmarks. If you want to give away things like tee shirts, it will mean that you will need to carry a large stock in various sizes.

There are plenty of companies online who specialise in promotional merchandise. Research them beforehand and source supplies carefully. Cost out each item per unit and remember to add on any possible shipping costs you will incur, both within the UK, and abroad. You can dispatch through Amazon, but they will charge you for that service and might end up making it unviable. You could invest in bulk buying. This will keep the unit price to its lowest, but it will mean you have to think about storage and that initial investment.

Think about how you are going to keep selling your merchandise beyond the limited marketplace of your book and the initial flurry of interest around its launch. Consider then the wider LGBTQ+ community. Would a tee shirt with your book cover or logo on it look completely out of place at Pride, or would it add something? Badges and pins are a popular way for people to unobtrusively show their support and allegiance for a cause or to state their own sexuality.

Merchandise is an interesting area to get into and there are many independent authors who successfully do it. Have a look at what they do for some ideas, but do the sums and talk to other people who have experience before you commit to anything.

18.4 Virtual Blog Tours

We often see well-known authors roll into town on yet one more sell-out stop on a traditional book tour, but is this a realistic option for promoting a new book from a lesser known, and especially, first-time self-published author?

If you can get an hour's slot at your local library or friendly bookshop in which to do a talk about your book, that is great, but for many, a virtual online book tour, in the form of written blogs, offers a better way of reaching many potential readers without having to go up and down the country with all the added expense and hassle that entails.

You might have seen authors posting schedules for their virtual book tours on social media. Instead of venues in different towns, these tours take place over a shorter time span, often around two weeks, and are hosted by different social media bloggers. The author's schedule gives details of the dates and online addresses for when the blogs go live.

As with anything, a blog tour doesn't just happen, it takes planning and building of relationships with the bloggers months in advance of the actual event. You should start thinking about pulling together a list of bloggers who might be willing to work with you, long before you have finished the final draft of your book.

Successful bloggers need content as much as you need publicity for your book, so don't be afraid to ask them to feature you. Search the internet for those who feature LGBTQ+ writers. Be specific in your online search, don't just look for generic 'book bloggers'. You want to find people who are primarily interested in talking to you about your LGBTQ+ topic. You might only come up with a handful, but make these your main focus. Research what these bloggers post, what their audience reach is, and how many followers and likes they get on social media. Do they review books? If so you will need to supply them with an ARC and factor in the time for delivery. What are their submission rules? Do they run competitions or give-aways?

Some popular book review bloggers are naturally inundated with requests and very often close their submissions for a time, and some will not look at independent authors at all.

Disregard any bloggers who are not especially active or do not have profiles on the same social media platforms you use. Like and follow all those who do. Start to interact with them by commenting on and liking their posts. Share as much as you can, especially if what they have posted is relevant to you and your book. When they comment back, keep the dialogue flowing.

Think also about where the blog is located in the world; is that audience relevant to your subject matter? Keep updated notes on your spreadsheet against each blogger you contact. Once you have established a list of your most wanted bloggers, look further afield to include others who may have a less obvious association with your LGBTQ+ topic.

Tips for building a blog tour:

- Tailor your pitch to the requirements of each blogger. Use your press release as a guide or email them a copy, but also include why you and your book will sit well with their blog. Tell them what you can offer them in return, in terms of your own social media reach, and anything else you might be able to link them into. For instance, you might be doing a talk and would be happy to mention their blog and point people in their direction.
- Don't talk about just your book if you are also involved in other LGBTQ+ projects or organisations. Tell them you are happy for them to include that information in the blog post as well.
- Ask them for any recommendations of other LGBTQ+ bloggers you might not have heard of.
- Try to build your blog-tour around a fixed timeframe. But first start by making enquiries around which date they can do.
- Aim to get at least one blogger to post something about you and your book on each day of your tour. Ideally you will get enough to fill a week or possibly two. But even just a few blogs spread out over a couple of weeks make perfect marketing material, so don't worry if you have not got a full two-weeks-worth scheduled in.
- Create a professional looking virtual flyer of the blog tour dates and promote it widely and regularly before and during the tour. Once the tour starts, ensure that you like, retweet, and comment on everything that's generated through each of the blogs.

Continue to nurture your relationships with these bloggers after your blog tour has finished so that you can reconnect with them again in the future. A blog tour might increase sales by a little or a lot, but whatever the effects, a good blog tour will definitely increase awareness of you and your book to a wider audience.

18.5 Reviews

Any pre-order reviews and every subsequent review thereafter of your book, particularly by those who have bought it and not free downloads, are an important part of your marketing toolkit and are vital in setting the algorithms into action. Widely quoted research by Brightlocal states that 'Positive reviews make 91% of consumers likely to use a business.' And when it comes to helping someone choose a new book to read, an upbeat five-star review is a positive nudge in steering them towards making that purchase.

Good reviews are like gold dust and should be posted all over your social media whenever you can.

You can find book reviewers on the internet who specifically review LGBTQ+ books. Almost all book reviewers are doing this in their spare time simply because of their love of books, so it is important to be grateful and to do whatever you can for them to 'pay back'.

Contact local book clubs and other online LGBTQ+ book groups to see if they would like to feature and read your book. Other groups such as you can find on Goodreads, and Facebook are great forums for picking up insider knowledge about book reviewers and bloggers other people have used or book clubs they can recommend.

You should expect at least one or two organic reviews when your book is first launched, if only from people you know, and there is no harm in asking readers for them, but you have to be careful if you are asking friends and relatives. For a potential customer, the biggest turn-off is to read a review clearly written by the author's nearest and dearest, since they are obviously going to write something glowing and give it five stars. If you are going to ask Aunty Mabel, make it clear that she must pretend she doesn't know you when she writes her review. If Amazon spots such a review and think it is not 'real' they can remove it.

It is perfectly okay, according to Amazon rules, to ask for reviews while running a free or discounted book promotion (a review of a discounted book, rather than a free one is better, because it counts as a 'Verified Purchaser'). You cannot, however, bribe someone for a review by offering a prize or money, or by threatening to remove them from your newsletter subscriber list, if you have one.

Encourage your readers of the value of reviews by reminding them how important it is to you that your book is recognised and read by as many people as possible. Push the point that many LGBTQ+ people won't hear about your book unless other people talk about it, and reviews on Amazon and elsewhere are vital for this communication.

Always have a link at the back of your book that takes the reader to your reviews page on Amazon. If they've read to the end and enjoyed the experience, they are more likely to follow the link, rather than go away and think about it.

Local papers and magazines will invariably be happy to review your book, if you provide them with an angle, the content, a free copy of the book, and a photograph of the book cover and of you. Check out their website, follow their guidelines and always approach the person responsible politely. Don't be afraid to give it a try. They need to fill their pages and are more approachable than you might think.

19. Telling *their* Story: Gireesh

Gireesh is a writer, poet, artist, translator, and LGBTQ+ activist from Tamil Nadu, south India. He was born in Nagercoil at the southernmost tip of the Indian continent and moved to Chennai at the age of 19 to find a job and to continue his studies.

He is the Festival Director of Chennai Queer LitFest and is best known for his Tamil book Vidupattavai published in January 2018; the first Tamil book written by an out gay person. His second book, a novel, is based on Vidupattavai. He has translated children's books from English to Tamil and was lyricist for a Tamil film based on the lives of Trans people. His articles on social issues from a LGBTQ+ perspective and creative works have appeared in various publications. Gireesh's writing focuses on dismantling masculinity and on the intersection of LGBTQ+ identities with caste, class and language.

He has travelled across Tamil Nadu training marginalized LGBTQ+ people on life skills and to oversee outreach programs. In 2015 he was selected as one of the change makers in the leading Tamil weekly *Kalamin Kaladichuvatil*. He continues to write and talk about the necessity of literary spaces to be inclusive of LGBTQ+ voices.

My first book was released in January 2018 at the 42nd Chennai Book Fair. Special guests introduced my book and for that one hour my whole body stood trembling. I had been going to that book fair for ten years by then. I had bought books by my favourite authors, and I saw those writers standing there at a distance. I almost passed out with fear, even though I wanted to get autographs from them.

After the publication of my book, someone asked *me* to sign a copy of my book they had bought. I never even thought this would happen in my life. To have my book published was something I had only dreamed of. It would be the first book in Tamil written by an out gay man in Tamil Nadu.

I was born in the year 1986 in Kanyakumari district of Tamil Nadu. I was born to a father who worked as a daily wage labourer and a mother who looked after the house and the children and raised a family by doing menial work to earn some extra income. I was the third of three children.

We lived in one of the six row houses in a housing compound. There was hardly any space inside the house to freely move around and my mother would not let me out to play as well. The houses had no electricity and everyone who lived in that housing compound were daily wage workers.

The person who lived next door drew promotional banners on cloth for a living. As a kid I enjoyed drawing, and during holidays I helped assist him in his work. He gave me the used paint brush and left-over paints for helping him. I used to draw on the walls of my house using those paints. Apart from painting I enjoyed reading too. I picked up the reading habit from my mother. The only recreation my mother had was to read and she made time for that.

With a minimum income, buying books was a luxury for our family. My mother would save a little money every week to buy a weekly magazine. I still vividly remember how my father would get it on Mondays when he returned from his work. After her daily chores, my mother would put us to bed and would read to us using the kerosene lamp. She would finish the magazine in one go. The rest of the week, she would share the stories she read with our neighbours. At times I used to lie on my mother's lap and listen to the stories. Half the stories were incomprehensible, but I always hoped that I would understand them once I grew up.

A few years later my father set up his own tea stall with the money he had saved. After school hours and in the holidays, I used to help him at the stall. The stall also sold sweets, savouries and biscuits which would be wrapped in paper when customers bought them. For wrapping, my father used to buy used books and magazines in bulk and store them in the stall. When I was bored at the stall and when business was lean, I would pick up a random book or magazine and read them when my father was not around. The tea stall was not successful, and my father returned to work for others, as a cook. Which meant I would again spend my free time inside the house as I was not allowed to go outside or play with boys of my age as my mother feared I would be spoiled.

By the time I was 15 I had partially realised my sexuality. I realised that I had more of an attraction to men but could not identify myself with the label 'gay' as I had not come across the term yet in my life. This created a whole lot of confusion about my gender identity, as I was taught that men should be attracted to women. If I was attracted to a man, what did that make me? At the same time, I had the opportunity to borrow books from the local community library. In one of those books, I found out about transgender women and for a while I thought I could be a trans person. Nineties India did not have many resources or discourse around gay rights. I gathered information on whatever little I came across in the mainstream magazines and newspapers.

Although I was constantly reading books, I never put any effort into writing as I was growing up. As a teenager all I wanted was to get out of the small town, and to achieve that I realised I had to find a job in the city. Soon after my diploma, I moved to Chennai in search of a job. For a short while I worked in an editing studio as an intern with no pay. By this time, I had also picked up on my drawing skills. A friend who saw my paintings suggested that I should apply for the fine arts college to get a formal degree in art. The following year I cleared the entrance exam of the College of Fine Arts in Chennai.

College life in the city was different from that in my town. I had also grown more comfortable with my sexuality around this time. I was more confident in meeting other gay men whom I connected with online, and I dated one guy I met through the internet. At those times, my writing skills were about writing letters and poems for him. When I was in the third year of the university, I broke up with him. Until then, the only audience for my writing was this guy I had dated. After the breakup I got the courage to share them with others. I read one of my poems in a Pride month LGBT event in Chennai in 2011. People who gathered for the event appreciated my work. That gave me a little confidence in myself about my writing.

After that I started allocating time for writing after college and the job I joined after university. I was aware that nothing can be done with praise once it's received, and I did not dare to show anyone everything I wrote. A couple of years later I hesitantly showed a few of my poems to a friend, who I would go on to date and live with still today, who immediately said that the poems were worthy to be published. Around 2013 there weren't many articles or literary works published in Tamil that centered on gay narratives. There weren't platforms that were accessible to everyone, especially those who spoke and wrote in Tamil.

I realised it was important to register and document queer events that happened in Chennai as the mainstream media was (is) not interested to bring our voices to the forefront. I started writing them and published them on various web portals (LGBTQ+ and ally run) whenever possible. I was one of the few people who was documenting LGBTQ+ issues in Tamil.

In 2017 my partner, Moulee, and my friend, L J Violet, started Queer Chennai Chronicles with the aim to highlight queer voices in literature and primarily bring diverse queer narratives in Tamil. They asked me to send my writings that

I had not published so far and compiled my first, and QCC's first book, *Vidupattavai* in Tamil. I was not confident and was anxious about how my writings would be perceived by cis-heterosexual readers. To reach a wider audience QCC partnered with the mainstream publication, Karuppu Prathikal, to publish the book. The idea was to reach as many readers as possible and to avoid boxing the book as just gay literature.

The book was released in January 2018 and my anxiety shot up. In the following weeks, famous writers and activists started writing a lot of good reviews about my book, and it was reviewed by popular newspapers. I was also invited to several book readings. All of this gave me a great deal of confidence. Above all, there have been many instances where young queer people reach out to me at Pride parades and on the internet telling me how my writings have given them confidence.

As much as my book was received well, my publishers faced a new hurdle in submitting the book for awards. The book did not fall into any category in the award section, but still, some people suggested my book had to be recognized, as it broke all the norms. This gave me the insight that it is not always important to adhere to what is laid out already, but it is important to break the existing moulds that define literature. I was able to see what Queer Chennai Chronicles envisioned, when my partner and my friends put my writing together. This new-found insight and confidence as a writer got me involved in future projects with QCC. With our collective experience, and by publishing the first Tamil book written by an out gay author, it enabled us to expand our literary forum and publishing efforts.

We decided to organize India's first queer literature festival in 2018 and launched various literary programs to encourage aspiring queer identified writers and translators. The idea was to bring the mainstream literary and queer literary spaces together to discuss and move ahead.

As much as the Tamil literary space was progressive, it was very much cis-heterosexual centric. There wasn't any effort to be inclusive of queer people or our narratives in the literary space. Post section 377, there seems to be a renewed interest from 'mainstream' publishers to publish queer narratives, but I realised that it was difficult for these editors to even understand gay narratives to do justice to the manuscripts sent to them. Most of them did not understand gay sub-culture and our stories were alien to them, and the few publishers who were ready tried to fit our gay narratives into hetero-normative narratives. This they also backed by saying that this is how the publishing business works.

Also, the social cultural aspect does not allow everyone who is writing to be visible. I am pretty much out, but when it comes to family it is complicated how Indian families see non-hetero relationships. My partner and I move around as a couple within the family and socially, but it is not directly talked about within the family setup. As an income source, writing cannot be a career option for everyone, especially those who do not have material backup. I have a day job which pays my bills and I make the time to pursue my passion in writing and publishing.

One of my dreams is to bring more diverse narratives by queer people through literature that will tell our stories to the world and eventually challenge the literary space that is too rigid for change. I realise this will take time, but I am confident that this will happen eventually.

Contact Gireesh via www.queerchennaichronicles.com

20. Presenting You, The Author

Smartphone technology enables communication in today's world to be more and more visual. It is immediate. When it comes to presenting and promoting your book, you need to think in a visually impactful way.

Social media platforms are ideal places for displaying your book marketing in the form of pictures, short promo videos and vlogs (a video version of a blog), or in a podcast series. Regularity and consistency are key in uploading content which should be quirky, interesting, educational and above all, entertaining. When people click on a video, they have to stop what they're doing and invest their time to watch it, so it needs to be the best you can create.

An informative video about your book, including an introduction by you, allows your audience to hear your voice and more importantly see your face. We are drawn to seek out human faces, and we learn to do this from birth. Putting your face to your book will build your author brand and increase its distinct uniqueness. However, this is not always possible when writing about sensitive and emotive LGBTQ+ issues. Think carefully before you commit to doing it; it might not be right for you at this time. Using a penname can help deflect some negative attention and protect loved ones, but if someone you don't want to, comes across your image and makes the connection, even with a penname, the cat will be well and truly out of the bag.

You do not need to spend a lot of money making a super-slick video, or have exceptional photographic skills. Most smartphones are equipped with perfectly adequate cameras. Fancy equipment and special lighting are not essential, but useful of course if you have them. For many vloggers being outdoors where anything can happen is a big part of what makes their videos so interesting. It might look like they've thrown it together in a few minutes, but they actually take hours of careful planning, filming and editing to get them to a slick, professionally finished film.

Don't be put off by the thought that no one's going to watch a video on social media made by you. They will if it grabs their attention. People need to get something from it and it needs to be in two minutes or less. Anything over that, they will get bored and move on.

Few people will watch your video if it's not liked and shared, and you will be extremely lucky if it happens to go viral. Whatever it is that makes a video go stratospheric is so much down to serendipity that it's really not worth worrying about. But if you like the idea of adding another skill set to your already growing repertoire; start small, find a good editing tool, and give it a go. This is how you will learn to get better.

Is it worth making a book promo video in terms of sales v cost?

Short video promos, like trailers are great marketing, but it is probably not worth spending money on this if you are doing it purely to drive sales. Consider, as well, the time you will need to spend to make even a short two-minute video.

Cutting costs to the minimum can eliminate the 'is it worth it' predicament. You can create your own book trailer on a smartphone or digital camera, and you can edit, add in a soundtrack, and voice-over using Movie Maker or a similar editing tool.

A book promo video doesn't normally feature the author. Instead, images of the book cover art are combined with dramatic music and exciting text and may include a voice-over. If you are considering vlogging, or a podcast series, this is where you can be the visible host and have the opportunity to showcase who you are, what you write about and what you support.

When we watch a video, particularly one with educational content, we believe the person who is speaking to us, and we believe they know what they are talking about. They need not be an expert, but we trust what they tell us. It takes just a split second for our brain to make that judgement about whether or not we trust someone: raised eyebrows, high cheekbones, and the amount of white visible in the eyes are all good indicators of trustworthiness, which makes sense because this is how we look when we smile. Beware of staring eyes, automaton-like, though. If you wear glasses, you might think about removing them if they reflect the light and obscure your eyes.

Having any face in a video will capture people's attention, but yours as the author, is the one they will want to see. Your face on screen will create familiarity and help build trust and understanding of your LGBTQ+ story and will hopefully translate into some book sales.

Here are a few tips to making a video:

- Make it compelling, both in sight and sound.
- Think about the background, and have a few well-chosen objects placed behind you to help tell your story.
- If filming outdoors, make sure the sun is not glaring on the camera and that background noise doesn't drown out or distract from what you are saying.
- If filming in your home, make sure you're not going to be disturbed. Remove family pictures from view. Don't let pets run around yelping, or kids trying to sneak in while you are in mid-flow (although there can be some comedic value when things go wrong).
- Be you. Be authentic, giggle, trip-up, but always recover with humility. Bloopers or outtakes at the end of the video can be fun and show your sense of humour.

- Write down the important things you want to say in big bold type so that it is easy to read, and pin it up just off camera. Never have this sheet on your lap because nobody wants to see the top of your head as you read.

One thing that puts people off appearing on video, or for some simply having their photo taken, is the feeling that they do not conform to some ideal of beauty. Humans are hardwired to respond to other human faces, but beauty per se is quite literally only skin deep. Imperfect, real people are engaging and memorable, and, as in our daily lives, the more we get to know someone the more their foibles and flaws become irrelevant. We instinctively build a rapport with those faces we see more of. Vlogging regularly will build that connection with your audience and promote your author brand recognition.

It is perfectly normal to feel apprehensive when confronted by an all-seeing camera lens. What will people think of me, what if I stutter and get my words mixed up, what if I go red and blotchy? These are common concerns we all share because we are social beings, and how others respond to us is important. However, when we see ourselves on video, we see the opposite of what we are used to seeing in the mirror and this appears odd to us. Likewise, we never normally get to appreciate our hand gestures and body language. All these things appear new and different when we see ourselves for the first time on video. Your quirky gesticulations or subtle tics might appear as irritating distractions, but in fact, the opposite is true. Being expressive with our hands makes us appear genuine and open.

Often when we are in situations that make us feel uncomfortable or vulnerable, we compensate by subconsciously making ourselves appear smaller, by hunching forward, crossing our arms in front of us or crossing our legs tightly as if we're building a physical barrier. To the viewer this can look like a nervous disposition or worse, that we're trying to hide something. Standing in front of the camera will help prevent this.

What you wear can make a big difference as well to people's perception of who you are. Wear clothes that are comfortable but reflect your brand image. Be aware of inadvertently promoting or advertising by staying clear of any logos or branded tee shirts. Avoid a high-fashion look. Trends change rapidly, and you don't want you and your video to look out of date in six months' time.

Colours, such as ruby red, emerald green, and sapphire blue, or gold and orange, are good for all different skin tones and complexions as they don't appear muted against most backgrounds. If you want to appear hard working, you might roll your sleeves up. If you want to look serious, wear a suit. If you want to look fun, wear something colourful.

If you are doing a series of vlogs or podcasts, stick to the same theme when it comes to what you wear on each episode. Don't one day wear formal workwear if on the previous video you were in a tee shirt, unless that's in the script.

The key to any good video performance is not to take yourself too seriously. The subject you want to talk about might require a certain amount of gravitas, but that shouldn't mean that you come across as wooden. The best way to overcome all the negative feelings is to keep doing it. Familiarity and practice will make the situation second nature. Breathe deeply and stretch your arms high in the air before you start. This will help your body to relax and slow down your heart rate.

Post your videos widely on social media, set up a YouTube channel, and hopefully people will share and like them. Ultimately, the more often you make and present your videos, the easier it will become, and you will find that people are receptive, warm, and genuinely interested in you and what you have to say.

20.1 Podcasts

Podcasts have become a hugely successful means of communicating with an audience and is now a mainstream alternative to listening to things that could only have been heard on radio talk shows before, but with added diversity. They offer the perfect forum for LGBTQ+ authors to talk about their books and their personal stories.

They are episodic series of digital audio, or video, lasting up to an hour or more, which the user can download at their convenience. Most are free, but some do have subscriber fees or require a subscription to another service. There are many LGBTQ+ specific podcasts and ones that feature writers of all diversities. You can search online for a list of the best ones.

The huge popularity in podcasts is due to the ease of access and the ability to listen, or watch in the case of video podcasts, wherever and whenever you like: in the car, on the train, out and about, sitting at the computer, or in bed.

Some have big production behind them and are hosted by big-name celebrities, but like any top radio or TV shows, these are not always the easiest to get onto as a guest. Often the best podcasts are those with a solo presenter or two otherwise unknown people chatting about topics they're passionate about and that resonate with their listeners: *Being LGBTQ Podcast* with Sam Wise, *Lost Spaces* with K. Anderson or *Story of a Storyteller* with Conor Bredin, are just a few.

Whichever podcast you are going to be on it is important to know as much as you can about it beforehand. Look at their website, social media, and the presenters. It's always good to put a face to the name.

Being interviewed on camera, (which is usually done via Zoom or Skype), is different to being just heard and you will need to think about things like body language and how you are projecting yourself.

Here are some tips to help give the best version of you in interview in front of the camera:

- It is important to be animated and not to look stiff. When we talk to someone in person, we don't just listen to what they are saying but we 'read' their facial expressions and body language too. The audience will be looking for these visual clues as well.
- Unless you are a truly experienced thespian, don't try to create a false persona. Even if you use a penname, that is not who you are. Be *you*. You cannot be fake in front of the camera.
- Never chew gum, suck sweets or eat. The occasional sip of drink is acceptable, especially if it is a long recording.
- Make sure you maintain eye-contact and keep your focus on the interviewer.
- If you are in a joint interview, keep still and maintain your attention on the interviewer when the other person is speaking. Don't start gazing around or fidgeting, because it will make you look disinterested. We've all seen that happen in Zoom meetings.
- Do not hold anything in your hands because you will unknowingly fiddle and that will make you look nervous.
- Don't slouch. Sit up straight and lean forward a little so that you appear interested in what the interviewer has to say. This will also help with your breathing by opening up your diaphragm.
- Sometimes things go wrong, be it technical, or human error. If anything happens let the

interviewer deal with it but show some humour at the situation. They can cut and edit later and may decide to include it to show your funny side.
- Always call the interviewer by their first name, be polite and well-mannered.
- Be upbeat and cheerful when you're first introduced; dependent, of course, on the severity of the subject matter and following conversation.
- Never give a simple yes or no answer. Elaborate and be enthusiastic and passionate about your subject. That's what people want to see. Sometimes, a well-timed yes or no answer can make for a dramatic pause and literally grab people's attention, but those moments are rare and should not be forced. Don't worry too much about the length of your answers. You can stop when you feel you have said enough, and the interviewer will be listening for such a pause to pose another question. Cuts and edits will be made to fit the airtime.
- If you need to include technical information, explain it in a way that can be easily grasped and understood. Have that information to hand if you think it might come up and you can even show it to the camera. It is quite legitimate to read something out if it is short and if you want the audience to really listen and understand the detail.

20.2 Radio

When we hear our own voice for the first time, we find it difficult to believe that this is how the world hears us. This is because the voice you hear in your head and recognise as yours, literally is that. You are the only person who will ever hear your voice like that because of the way sound travels through the air, as opposed to the combination of sounds coming from your mouth into your ear with the additional vibrations through your skull. You might think you sound strange when you hear yourself speak on radio or another audio recording, but you sound perfectly normal to everyone else because that's how they hear you. The way we sound is just part of who we are. People hearing your voice for the first time, won't be listening to the sound you're making, but what you have to say.

Don't worry about sounding nervous either. Everybody has to deal with their nerves in such an unusual situation and the audience will sympathise with that feeling. In fact, they will warm to you knowing that you are not used to this sort of thing, and you will come across as genuine. People would rather hear real nervous tension to someone who sounds false and answers all the questions as if they've learned a set of verbatim answers they cannot deviate from. Whatever you do just keep talking, never answer with a monosyllabic 'yes' or 'no'. The presenter will do their utmost to make you feel comfortable and they want to have a conversation, but also to ask the sorts of questions their listeners will be interested in hearing your answers to.

Doing radio interviews is still a lucrative way to promote your book and talk about your LGBTQ+ topic and there are numerous LGBTQ+ specific radio stations such as Gaydio, Gorgeous FM, Pride Radio and ShoutOut Radio. Getting yourself onto mainstream national radio is as much down to serendipity and bravado, as it is having a captivating and unique personal story. Most national broadcast radio shows will contact you if they want you on, but local or independent radio stations are often more accommodating because they cannot fill their airtime with celebrity guests.

To approach a radio station, look on their website for contact details and email them your press release with a good reason why you would make an interesting guest to have on their morning chat show or evening discussion panel. Having a book released will not in itself be a sufficient reason, but your unique LGBTQ+ story might. In that case, know the audience the show attracts and have some knowledge of the presenter.

Radio shows are very different to podcasts, in that the interview will invariably be live on-air and consequently time-limited, perhaps only a few minutes between tracks or before a news update at the top of the hour, or dissected between adverts.

Most producers prefer it if you can use a landline rather than a mobile, to avoid losing the signal. Whichever phone device you use, make sure that you will not be interrupted. If you're using a landline, turn off your mobile phone once the producer has made contact. Leave it on until then in case they are having trouble getting through to you. Make sure that doors and windows are closed, and pets are shut away so they cannot disturb you. Do not put your phone on speaker as this will pick up background noise.

All the arrangements will be confirmed with you beforehand by email. They might also call you to make sure you are confident and able to speak over the phone and then call you on the day a few minutes before you go on-air. Sit in a fixed chair, not one that swivels or rocks, and keep your mouth near to the receiver. They will then set the levels so that you come through loud and clear. After the track playing has finished, you will hear the presenter make their introductions and they will speak directly to you. Remember that you only have a limited time to get everything you want to say across, so keep your answers relatively short. At the end of the interview, the producer will speak to you, thank you, and say goodbye. That's it.

If you are invited to go to the studio you will find there is a distinct difference between local and national radio stations and how they work. Local stations tend to be far more relaxed, and you might be taken into the studio during the last song having already met and had a brief chat with the presenter beforehand.

National radio stations have a lot of producers and different staff doing all sorts of things. There is a distinct buzz in the air. On arrival you'll be taken to the greenroom where you'll meet other guests appearing on the show. Just before you're due to go on, one of the show's producers will take you through to the studio where the presenter will be talking live to the audience about the next topic they're about to discuss and who they are going to be talking to. You might be forewarned about the direction of the questions, but generally not. Once you're in the seat and settled, sitting up close to the mic, the presenter will introduce you and fire the first question.

The time will go very quickly and before you know it, the next track will be playing. You'll then have a moment or two to say your goodbye's before you'll be taken down to reception and find yourself back on the street again. You'll feel exhilarated and ready to conquer the world.

Always email the presenter the next day to thank them for having you on their show and publicise it on your social media. If people have missed your radio debut, they can always catch up via the internet. Post a link and tell them at what point in the show they can hear your interview (how many minutes in).

Here are a few tips when it comes to doing radio interviews:

- Make sure you have a glass of water nearby in case you dry up or have a cough. Always apologise if you cough or sneeze on-air.
- If you're on a live show, taking questions from listeners, write their name down so that you can refer to it. Such phone-ins will likely have a time-delay so that if something untoward happens, the producer can pull the plug before it goes out live.

- If you are invited to the studio for a face-to-face interview, make sure you get there at least an hour before you're due to go on-air. Do check in with reception so that they know you've arrived, and for your own peace of mind that you're in the right place.
- List and memorise the main points you want to get across. The absolute priority is the title of your book and where people can get hold of it. Don't keep repeating the title ad nauseum but do make sure you use it when you can in the conversation. The presenter will mention you and your book in their introduction and at the end, but it's always good to give it a boost in your own voice too. This reinforces the link between you and your book.
- Practise answering the most likely questions that will come up. You could get a friend to call you on the phone and go through a few questions as if it were for real to help boost your confidence.
- Invariably, a curveball question will be thrown in towards the end if there is time. Don't panic. Answer as clearly as you can, and if you flounder just steer things back to where you're more comfortable. If you really cannot think of an answer, say that's something you've never been asked before and that you really don't have a definitive answer for, or perhaps they'd like to invite you back on the show at a later date to talk about that point again in detail.
- If you're not sure what they mean by a question, get them to repeat it or to clarify what they're getting at. Always be honest in your answers. You are not on trial; their purpose is to make you sound as interesting as possible. If you realise you've made a mistake in your answer, say so. People will

appreciate your honesty; they don't want to hear you give a politician's answer.
- Answer the question that is being asked, don't be tempted to backtrack to a previous question because you don't feel you answered it fully enough. The audience will want to hear what else you have to say and not go over what's already been discussed.
- Dropping in a few choice statistics or unpicking common LGBTQ+ myths will strengthen your position and make everyone aware that you know what you're talking about.
- If there is something topical going on in the news at the time, try and tie that in if you can, but only if it is relevant.
- It is always good to get in one short story or anecdote.
- Don't mumble, speak clearly and in your own accent, and try not to umm and ahh too much.

20.3 Giving A Talk

Talking about ourselves, especially in front of strangers, makes many of us feel incredibly awkward. Anyone who's had to talk about their book, whether in a crowded room or in a one-to-one conversation, will know that dreadful feeling when someone asks an obscure question you'd never thought of before, or even something simple you cannot find the words to answer. The thing to remember is that we cannot know everything and be expected to recall every piece of information and research at any given moment. What people really want to hear about is you and your story.

Sometimes even the simplest of questions, like 'why did you write your book?', seem difficult to answer because it is so obvious to us, but for the person asking, it is a genuine unknown. Replying truthfully is not about self-promotion or stroking your ego, but rather about retelling your wealth of experience, and that is something you should most certainly never be ashamed of.

Another thing that often stops people from talking openly about themselves or their book, is the thought of being immediately judged for the way we speak, the way we stand and hold ourselves; where everything about us, everything personal, is suddenly up for criticism and scrutiny. It can be so overwhelming that we can enter a state of panic. This is part of our evolutionary defence, the flight or fight mode. We all know what that feels like: racing heart, tightening of the chest, sweats, constricted breathing, dry throat, stammering, even forgetting your own name let alone being able to string together a few words to make a sentence. It is a horrible feeling.

How, then, do people ever manage to stand on a stage and speak into a microphone and make their voice even more audible for those staring back at them?

Firstly, there are two distinct ways of speaking to an audience. The first is 'presenting'. This is where you talk in a knowledgeable and authoritative way on a particular topic, imparting the information in an easily digestible and understandable format and style. This is often done as a PowerPoint presentation, where slides are accompanied with commentary. Presenting in this way, the speaker is confined to having to know the information and be able to answer questions that might be very specific. There is very little room for error but might be ideal for you if you're someone who works well in a controlled setting.

The other form of speaking in public, and one which is ideal for authors and their books, is to give a talk either solo or as part of a discussion panel. Both being much less rigid and involves more engagement with the audience. For a talk to work well, the audience needs to leave the venue feeling they have participated, contributed, and learned something from the event. People attend book events because they are interested in hearing from the author. You, the author. Anybody can give a presentation about LGBTQ+ issues if they know enough, but only you can give a talk or add your experience to a panel of experts, and that's why people will turn up to hear you speak. When you start to talk about you and your personal experiences you will realise that there is nothing you cannot answer. Knowing that alone can boost your confidence no end, and in time and with familiarity, your fears of speaking in public will diminish.

How can we lessen those feelings of fear when we have them?

A lot of the panic we feel comes from our breathing and most of the symptoms are brought on by not breathing properly. We tend to pant, taking in little breaths that don't get down into the depths of the lungs, and so our bodies become starved of oxygen, which adds to the sense of panic and light-headedness.

To stay calm, try breathing slowly, steadily filling your lungs and expanding your chest. Experience what this feels like by putting your fingers just below your sternum on your diaphragm and breathe in so that your fingers are pushed away from you. Or, place your hands on your sides just below your ribcage and breathe in and out and feel your body expanding and deflating with air. In the minutes before you speak to the audience, focus on your breathing and you will feel calmer.

Speak a little deeper and slower if you can. This too will help regulate your breathing. Don't worry about tripping over words, getting them round the wrong way, or even completely forgetting what you are saying. This is normal, the audience knows that, and they will wait for you to correct yourself and resume. Even professional interviewers and speakers do this all the time. When they make a fluff, they stop, take a breath, and start again. The worst thing you can do is to search for what you want to say on a piece of paper in front of you. No matter how large the font, you won't be able to register what it says. Put the paper down, look to the back of the auditorium, above the audience, breathe, and if you still can't regain what you were saying, ask the person to repeat the question, or say 'where was I?' or 'I've completely lost my thread.' People will see your pain and they don't want you to fail, someone will pipe up to help you.

Always be yourself. Remember your brand image and be understated and comfortable in what you wear. This way you will be remembered for what you say and not how you look. In reality, once you've hooked your audience with your emotive LGBTQ+ story, they'll soon forget what you are wearing.

Here are some tips on preparing for and giving a talk:

- Make a plan. How broad will your talk be? Tell the audience what will be covered.
- Get the audience on your side by opening gently with something about the weather or the traffic in town.
- Check out the location. Do you need a projector? Will you need to rearrange the seating? Is there sufficient parking and is it nearby? Will it be a ticketed event and who will do the job of checking people in at the door?
- Equipment will always fail at the most inappropriate time. If a slide does not come up in the correct order, stay calm, and go back or jump forward to the next one. Involve the audience in the misfortunes of working with technology. It's the uncomfortableness of these situations, and we've all seen it happen, that the audience feels and is relieved when the presenter puts it all right or turns

the situation around, that gets the spontaneous applause.
- Focus on the key points you want to deliver. Whatever happens, you must talk about these and what you hope others will learn.
- Don't worry that you're repeating something you've said a thousand times before, to this audience it will be fresh, and the more confident you sound speaking those words, the more riveting the audience will find them.
- When answering questions from the audience, always bring it back to you and your experience, so that your audience can connect with you.

21. Websites/Blogs

Many authors have a website or a blog. They are essentially the same thing; online websites and blogs are comprised of one or more pages of content. The difference between the two is that blogs are updated regularly with articles written by the author. A one-stop website is a virtual shop for everything associated with the author and may not include content writing. With the rise in popularity of social media platforms to communicate with their audiences, many authors now find setting up and maintaining a website an unnecessary additional task and expense.

If your budget includes provision for a website, then the advantages of having such an online presence, where everything about you and your book is located, can outweigh any disadvantages of not having one, and especially if you have several books. A website can offer anyone with a casual, or professional interest in you and your book, the opportunity to link to your social media pages, read a blog (if you write one), learn about who you are through your bio, email you, find out about other work you're involved in, read articles you've feature in, listen to podcasts, interviews, and watch your videos. The aim of a good working website is to embrace and optimise every casual looker who lands there. It should work for you by getting your voice heard and increase your book sales.

The main thing to remember is you must keep your website relevant and updated regularly.

It can be time-consuming to manage, but if your website is not current and up to date it will soon look and feel tired, giving the impression that you have either lost interest in it or have nothing new to offer your audience. Algorithms will quickly lose interest too.

When creating a professional website, it should reflect your book but also who you are and what you want to present to your audience. Think of it in terms of the visualisation of your brand. From the user's point of view, your website should be clear and easy to navigate around.

When someone browsing lands on your website, they will have a number of immediate questions:

- Where am I?
- What can I do here?
- How do I get started?
- What is keeping me here?

Chiefly, people look for familiar clues that will help them, such as buttons and standard page headings that they instantly recognise. Don't try to stand out by being quirky, it will only confuse and make people leave your page before they've even got started.

It is up to you what content you put on your website, but a typical author website will usually have the following pages, accessible via tabs that run across the top bar and are named:

Homepage

This page is the customary place people arrive at after clicking a link or searching for you online. They will look at your homepage and will judge how it appears and how they feel about going further in a matter of milliseconds. You might get a few seconds more attention if they are looking to find something specific, like your book, or how to contact you, but someone who is generally browsing will only keep looking in the time it takes to turn a page in a real book. Google research suggests that this window of opportunity is certainly no longer than ten seconds. Therefore, your homepage needs to be immediately effective, reflect what your website is about and inform instantly where they need to go to get the information they want.

Think of the homepage as opening the door into your shop. Anyone entering will scan the shelves and try to establish where they should look to get what they're interested in, and be able to do that straightaway. They won't want to bother if they have to work through a cryptic maze of undecipherable tabs and paragraphs of text to get them there.

The challenge for your website is to convince potential readers that your book, which is what you want to lead them to, is utterly different from anything else they will have seen before, and that it has helped other LGBTQ+ people just like them.

Your website needs to tell a cohesive story and have a natural flow that leads to the end goal.

The homepage should not be about you. It is about emotionally connecting your customer with the prospect of what lies beyond. Some homepages reveal so little that you are forced to delve deeper. There is a fine line with this approach as it can be off-putting if it feels like you're being sucked into a rabbit hole or that the site is trying to hide something. It can work very effectively with a beautiful and alluring image that reveals as little as necessary, but enough to show that you understand what your visitor wants.

Books

If you have several books, it might be a good idea to have a drop-down list with a separate page for each one. On each dedicated page, have an image of that book's front cover. You could include the back cover too if you want people to read the back-of-book blurb. You should definitely include a synopsis, but don't make it too long, just a paragraph or two. Include a couple of meaningful review quotes if you can. Have the book's details; the format it can be purchased in, number of pages, ISBN, and RRP. You might also include a Read Sample link, or an audio book sample if the book is available in this format. Always include a red 'Buy' button that links straight to your book on your online bookstore. This is known as creating a 'call to action' that hopefully translates into a purchase.

Whenever you link to your website via articles or posts, it should always be to this page, or if you have multiple books, to the most recent one because that's the book most people will be looking for. Linking from other places to your website in this way is known as the 'landing page' and should be highly optimised for search engines to find. That means using words and phrases in the content that can be easily recognised, picked up and ranked by search engines such as Google. Search engine optimisation (SEOs) is a huge topic and there are plenty of places to look online if you want to know more about it, but suffice it to say, for LGBTQ+ authors interested in letting people know about their books, gay language and terminology should be liberally sprinkled in the content. However, worrying excessively over SEOs will probably not make that much difference to warrant it.

About

This page is where you *can* talk about yourself. Write a short biography, and how you came to write your book, what inspired you and, importantly, the uniqueness of your position that gives you the absolute authority to tell your LGBTQ+ story. Keep the paragraphs short and snappy. Give just enough information so that the reader will want to go and purchase your book to find out more.

On this page too, you can have a picture of yourself if that is appropriate for you. Don't use a holiday snap or a cropped group photo. If you can, always go with a professionally taken portrait or one that looks like it was taken in a studio. You should ideally be smiling, as this will engage the viewer. This image will be the one that journalists and bloggers will use, so it must be sharp focused and of good quality.

Blog or Articles

If you are going to write a regular blog, have a dropdown list in date or subject order. Start with the most recent blog at the top of the list. You might include vlogs as well under a sub-heading. Include social media 'Share' buttons on each article so that people can post them elsewhere.

Media

This is the page to put all the radio and podcast interviews you've done and any other media articles, such as newspapers and magazines you've appeared in. Also, YouTube videos you've guested on and links to your own podcast if you have one. Offer yourself for interview or to be a guest on panel discussions. Include a contact email and message box or a link to your contact page.

Contact

The contact page is where you can invite people to email you with their questions about you and your book. Use link buttons to your social media at the bottom of all your pages, but here you can make it clearer with an instruction, 'Follow me on my social media @ ... I love to connect with other LGBTQ+ writers and I always follow back.'

If you have a newsletter provide a sign-up box here. State how regularly your newsletter will be sent out and what they can expect to get from it. This will link to your Mailchimp (or other mailshot provider), and automatic subscriber emails will be generated. Many websites now include a 'pop-up' that asks for the visitor's name and email details to join their newsletter mailing list.

Always avoid having pages that look cluttered, instead have lots of white space. Stay away from sponsored pop-up ads: they can be quite irritating and confusing for the reader trying to look at something or find their way around.

Generally, stick to using black typeface on a white background. You might think that having something different will make your website look more interesting and individual, but others might struggle.

Your website should have a bold and easily searchable name, preferably your author name. The domain provider will let you know if your choice has been used before. You can choose between having a .co.uk, or .com website. Once you register your website name, this is then known as the domain name.

21.1 What Is The Difference Between .co.uk And .com?

Traditionally, .coms were the preference of international big business and .co.uk meant that your business was UK based rather than international in its market reach. On deciding between .co.uk or .com, firstly you need to have identified your core audience and where they live (see sub-chapter: 16.4 Defining Your Typical Customer). Many people feel a sense of loyalty towards UK companies who use .co.uk, so if your target audience is primarily UK based that might be worth considering. With .com companies it is not always possible to know straight away where they are in the world. However, if you intend to aim your book at the worldwide market, a .com domain might work better for you, as international consumers might not come across a .co.uk address in search engine rankings outside the UK as easily as a .com address.

You could purchase both. The yearly cost is around ten pounds for a .com domain and a few pounds less for a .co.uk, which you pay to the hosting company.

Virtually every word in the English language has already been registered to a domain name, as well as many made up words and people's names. If you are not going to use your name, penname, or book title as your website address, you will need to consider very carefully what you call your website. How easy will it be for people to find and what combinations of LGBTQ+ words or phrases will they likely use to search for pages on your given subculture or topic? People invariably only look at the first page of options Google or other search engines offer up, so it is very important that your website appears on that first page.

Once you have registered your domain name, the next thing you need for your website is a 'benefit rich' headline with 'added curiosity'. For example, 'Coming Out, it isn't easy. I did it, and I'll show you how you can too.' People would know immediately that they'd come to the right place for advice or guidance on this issue. Again, think about your book and what people will search for to get them there.

There are plenty of online suppliers you can use to set up your website and they have numerous design templates to make the process easy. Platforms such as GoDaddy or WordPress, and others, offer off-the-shelf, ready to go, websites. Look at their pricing structures and what you will get for your money. Does it include an email address, for instance? Will you be paying a monthly fee or a one-off annual charge for the hosting? While the cost might be inexpensive on a monthly basis, take into account that over years the cumulative cost could outweigh the benefits. It might be better to pay for a one-off web design package through a small independent designer and have them host your domain name for a small annual charge. It is well worth doing some research into.

It is also worth remembering that while website design platforms have many styles to choose from, when it comes to creating your web pages, having to do it yourself is still not easy. Unless you have some knowledge of graphic design it can lead to an eclectic and difficult to fathom website that might end up putting people off.

Your website, like all your other social media, should be on brand. Look at other LGBTQ+ author websites and take them as a starting point, but come up with something better and that is totally yours.

22. Telling *their* Story: Helen Dale

Helen Dale lives in Salford, Manchester. She identifies as female with a transsexual history, and, she says, 'I'm old enough to remember the Queen's Coronation and black and white TVs with nine-inch screens.'

My early career was in public relations, advertising and marketing; writing leaflets, press releases, advertisements, and proofreading others' work. I eventually ran my own marketing services company. All experiences that proved useful for my creative writing.

I identified as a transvestite until my fifties (cross-dressing as I saw it at the time), then going through long periods of purging. This is common amongst trans people; stopping dressing or the transition process. For me, these periods of denial were brought on by disasters that happened in my life that I saw as punishment from God for breaking his law about men wearing women's clothes. I would get rid of all of my female things; in the first instance throwing everything into the Thames off Vauxhall Bridge.

During one of these purging periods, I got married and had a daughter.

In 1994, my business had been hit by the recession and I started temping on a power station project. That led to a contract in North Wales and visits to Manchester for the Northern Concord TV/TS support group and going out around the Gay Village on a Saturday night. Chatting to the other members of the group, I realised I had much more in common with the transsexual members than the TV's and began to wonder if I might be TS myself.

I started to live 24/7 as Helen to see if I got bored with being female full-time. Prior to this the longest I'd spent 'en femme' had been a weekend.

At that time, I had a website and kept an online diary (I guess you'd call it a blog these days) in which I wrote about how I came out as trans to my family and friends. I also wrote a number of short stories for the Northern Concord group magazine and started to write a novel then entitled *Trojan Lady*. Fearing that I'd be lucky to get another job if I did transition, I also started training as a counsellor.

A second work contract never materialised, and I had to go back to work in a computer workshop as a male. I would wake each morning and think 'I just can't do this any longer, pretending to be a man'. Having lived full time before returning to work and having felt totally natural during that period, I knew that transition was right for me. I started treatment with the private psychiatrist that most UK trans people used if they didn't go via the NHS. When my work became aware that I was going to transition, my contract with them was terminated.

This was in 1998. As far as the family went, my wife and I had effectively separated by then and I waited until my daughter had completed her university degree before I told her.

I went with a group to see the Rocky Horror Picture Show. I was, inevitably, dressed in basque, stockings and high heels and made up to the nines. During a phone call later with my still then, wife, I mentioned that I'd been to the show, which in itself surprised her as I was, as far as she was aware, a total stick-in-the-mud with totally straight values. I told her it was sixties music, and she knew how I liked that era (it wasn't actually but she didn't challenge me). When I spoke to my daughter she asked 'Did you dress up? No, I don't suppose you did,' sounding disappointed.

When, I told her I did, she exclaimed, 'What, stockings and suspenders and all that? Did anyone take any photographs?'

The next time we met at her mum's the subject of the Rocky Horror Show photographs was raised.

'Have you got them with you?' asked my daughter.

I suggested that they should sit down to look at them. Time had run out. With my heart in my mouth, I passed them both the pictures of me in my outfit with my hair and make-up done.

They laughed. And laughed and laughed.

'You think it's funny me being dressed as a woman?' I asked quietly.

'Of course,' was the response.

I took a deep breath. 'I do it all the time,' I said. 'I'm a transvestite, here's some other photos of me.'

My wife was stunned, my daughter said, 'Cool'.

There was a long question and answer session covering the usual topics:

'How long have you been TV?' All my life, though it had been during a purge stage that we had met and married.'

'How had you hidden everything?' In the garage.

'Are you going to have the op?' Maybe, I don't know at the moment what will happen.

'Are you gay?' I don't fancy men and I have no idea how I will feel in the future due to the effects of hormones. At that moment I thought I'd probably turn out to be a lesbian.

'Why didn't you say anything earlier?'

I didn't understand it myself and could not expect my wife to accept something I felt disgusted about. By the time I realised that it was nothing to be ashamed of, I was living away and I felt it was best to wait until our daughter had finished her degree.

It was scary telling everyone. So many trans people lose all their friends and family at this stage. I was fortunate. My daughter was immediately accepting and everyone else that mattered eventually accepted my decision.

I was offered the very first job I had an interview for as Helen, with Greater Manchester Probation as IT Customer Services Manager. When I joined them in November 1999,

I was their first openly trans employee. I offered any help I could on trans issues and started to provide training workshops in addition to my official job. In 2000, I joined LAGIP – the probation service LGBT staff association. At that time, it was for Lesbian and Gay members only, but I persuaded them to extend the criteria to include Transgender and Bisexual members too. I served on the committee from 2000 until my retirement in 2015, including as Chair.

The year after my surgery, I had a yachting holiday in Greece (sailing has always been my sport). I was on my own so I was taking pot-luck as far as other members of the crew were concerned. Heading for the airport, I worried about their reaction but wasn't about to turn back. In fact, it never proved to be a problem; on the contrary, I was always invited to join with others for meals and I don't think anyone realised my history until I told them.

I joined a social group called Spice, an all-inclusive group, who do a fantastic range of different activities and holidays. I'd go into the office on a Monday morning and colleagues would ask resignedly 'So, what did you do *this* weekend?'

'Oh, I flew a jet and did a loop-the-loop and a roll,' I might answer. Or fire-eating or driving a tank. They'd roll their eyes and say, 'You should write your autobiography.' So, I did. I called it *A Tale of Two Lives: A funny thing happened on the way to the Palace*. The subtitle is a reference to receiving an award at Buckingham Palace.

I probably broke every rule in the book as far as autobiographies are concerned. Looking back, it's probably a bit too factual and not enough about how I was feeling. I don't think this is surprising. I grew up in a time when men didn't show their emotions and that attitude had been well ingrained in me. Most of the writing I'd done to that point had been technical with emphasis on getting the facts out and not padding with adjectives. I also had to decide whether to write it 'warts and all', revealing information I wasn't proud of as well as my achievements. I felt uncomfortable sharing that, but I knew it was important to be honest. I just hoped my family and friends wouldn't think less of me because of it.

The other aspect that might have caused me discomfort was writing about a childhood in a different gender and seeing photographs of me as a boy. That's certainly a big problem for many trans people. However, I'd actually dealt with this during a counselling course residential weekend when we had to talk about our childhood. I could look at it quite dispassionately.

I found it helpful to create a skeleton of dates and events and was glad that I'd been a bit of a hoarder and that my mum had sent me material from my childhood including school reports.

My aim with my book was to produce something that helped others to understand what it had meant for me to be trans and the impact it had had on my life – good and bad. I didn't want it to just be a story of struggles but to show that being trans is simply a part of my life, it doesn't define me. Maybe it would also help others going through the process to avoid some of the mistakes I made and see that there is light at the end of the tunnel.

I launched *A Tale of Two Lives* at my work leaving do. I then discovered how to publish on Amazon, and it was relatively easy. Seeing and handling a printed copy of my autobiography was a real thrill.

After that I wrote a book based on the trans awareness workshops I'd been providing since 2000, called *Understanding Gender Variance*. While I was drafting my autobiography, I came across a number of my files from the 1990s including the diary I'd kept when I first moved to Manchester and some short stories I'd written. I added a few other incidents and created an anthology I entitled *Transgender Tales: Adventures and Misadventures on the Journey from Transvestite to Transsexual*.

As I wrote my book, *A Tale of Two Lives*, it brought back other memories. One of the incidents I remembered was a trip to Bournemouth when I was 19. I'd caught the train from Waterloo and changed in the toilets at the end of the corridor, putting on an orange bikini under my skirt and top. In Bournemouth, I walked along the seafront, took the Sandbanks ferry across to the beach and dunes at Studland, where I swam and sunbathed. As I lay there, I noticed a guy watching me, so I quickly dressed and left. I thought about this and realised that this could be a great start for a novel. What might have happened if I hadn't noticed the guy watching me? What if he'd approached me? What if he didn't mind that I was trans? I started writing a novel, *Summer Dreams,* set in 2003 when the Gender Recognition Act was going through parliament. I also wanted to get away from the stereotypes of trans individuals only being victims, fetishists, sex workers or criminals and of story lines that focus on the erotic. Certainly, my books include trans people who fall into most of these categories and there is sex, but I hope it's appropriate to the plot and not just to titillate.

Apart from writing, since retiring, I've been volunteering with Diversity Role Models, going into schools to talk about homophobic, biphobic and transphobic bullying. I also continue counselling and providing workshops on trans issues.

Helen Dale can be contacted via her website at www.helendaleauthor.info Her books are available through Amazon.

23. Social Media

Statistics on social media usage provide fascinating data on the way our lives have changed since Facebook was first introduced in 2004. Today, we all understand the reach and potential of utilising social media to increase our book sales and interact with potential customers. But which social media should we concentrate on using, or is the scattergun approach better?

People's usage of different networks varies. Platforms such as Facebook focus on creating communities by sharing things between family members, friends, and social groups. Other networks such as Twitter have a different focus and are about communicating rapidly in what is known as microblogs, or better known on Twitter, as *Tweets*.

Think of the difference between these networks as something like talking to a group of people you know, (though, of course, you won't actually know many of them), in the case of Facebook, and talking to work colleagues from different departments, in the case of Twitter. In our real lives, when we socialise with different groups, we unwittingly adopt different, and appropriate façades of ourselves for those different groups. Think in these terms when you are deciding which social networks you want to operate on and the tone you wish to adopt on each platform. Ask yourself the questions: who uses this network, what kind of people do I want to encourage to 'Like' and 'Follow' me, and what aspects of myself as an LGBTQ+ author, do I want to expose?

The point is that social media can help you to reach your specific audience in a way that would not have been possible just a few years ago. The downside is that you are a very, very small fish in a pond the size of the Atlantic Ocean. What is certain though, is that by not having an author page on Facebook or a Twitter account, a Pinterest scrapbook or LinkedIn page, or some other social media presence, nobody in the world will hear about you or your book outside your small circle of friends and close family.

The fact that you are writing about LGBTQ+ issues, which ultimately you want to share with and help as many other people as possible, means that you should absolutely use social media as a marketing tool and promotional platform because that is where you will find LGBTQ+ individuals, and groups run by and for your community.

Don't be frightened by the vastness of social media. Keep in mind your typical customer profile and look at each platform and see if it fits what you are trying to do. For instance, is the platform based on photo sharing? If so, does your book demand a lot of imagery and will you be able to post regularly? Do you want to be able to upload longer articles or short, pithy posts? Is your audience at the younger end of the scale and more used to viewing short videos?

Aim to focus on one or two social media sites and use them voraciously.

23.1 Facebook

Facebook is still the market leader when it comes to social media, and it was the first platform to surpass one billion registered accounts. It is now well beyond two billion.

It is good for text, images, and video posting, and for promotions such as local events, and building your LGBTQ+ community through its groups.

To set up a Facebook Author Page you must have a personal Facebook account first. If you do not already have one, go to Facebook.com/pages/create.

Whatever your topic for your LGBTQ+ book, there will undoubtedly be a kindred group already on Facebook, and, if not, you could set one up yourself. This can be a public or private group, and allows people to interact and discuss their common experiences and your book.

Growing your author page followers can be a slow and organic process. Every time someone new likes one of your posts, make sure you invite them to follow the page too. You can also invite your friends to follow, encourage them to spread the word, and share your posts at every opportunity. Let your audience know that when they like or follow your page, they should tick the 'See First' preference on the 'pages' tab. This will inform the algorithms that your page is important to them.

The trick, as with any social media, is to keep your content coming with regular posts and to create as much interaction as possible with people who like and comment on them. This will slowly start to build a buzz around you and your book, and what you stand for.

Having 500 followers seems to be the first magical algorithm switch-on number, but the way that Facebook's algorithms operate means that some days you will see that your posts have reached more people than on other days and there doesn't appear to be a reason for this. Facebook is very guarded about how its algorithms work and trying to understand them is probably a non-starter as they are regularly tweaked and changed.

Fake profiles from click-farms will 'like' your page and posts simply to make their own profile page look legitimate. Do not engage with them. If a gorgeous looking guy or girl pops up out of nowhere, likes your page, and says 'hi', just think for a moment. Take a look at their page, is there any history on there? How many followers do they have? Are they based in a faraway country? If so, just ignore them, and be thankful that they are at least boosting the number of likes your page gets.

Delete unfavourable or trolling comments and block the profile as quickly as you can. This applies to all social media. Do not engage in a war of words with worthless people. Just get rid of them. If, however, someone comments favourably, always comment back. It will make them feel just as good as their comment made you feel and the algorithms like this kind of back-and-forth conversation.

To encourage people to 'like' and 'follow' your page, you need to be setting off the addictive nature of the brain's endorphins with every click and scroll. Use a 'Call to Action' button to link people to your online book platform to purchase a copy or to your website to sign up to your newsletter (if you have one). Don't overdo the selling however, that will just put people off.

Facebook works well for connecting with people in other LGBTQ+ groups, but you should also like and join other groups that might be relevant to your subject, and be active in them. These groups need not necessarily be about books or specifically aimed at the LGBTQ+ community and can include other interests you might have. You will probably find that your target audience will be interested in many similar things to you. Read each group's terms and conditions before joining. Don't plug your book all the time, just engage with people, and let them know who you are and where they can find your author page.

Another way you can promote your book is to do a live Facebook Q&A session. Include some prizes and give-aways. Publicise this event in advance and get people to 'sign up' to say if they are attending. This is a numbers game, and can be a lot of work on your part for very little return. It will not be effective if you cannot get any more than one or two friends to join you. Have a clear idea about what you're going to talk about, nobody wants to watch somebody rambling on, filling time between incoming questions, and what happens if nobody asks a question? If you're nervous about doing this on your own there's no reason why you could not do it as a small group, perhaps with other LGBTQ+ authors or relevant individuals and experts who have an interest in your topic and might encourage a bigger audience attendance.

Facebook implemented some algorithm changes in 2018 which were intended to allay people's concerns that they were being bombarded with stuff that they didn't want to see. Facebook's objective is to always factor in ways of keeping people engaged for longer periods in each scrolling session so that advertisers see the benefit of millions of captive participants. The results of the changes made were that people were shown fewer links directing them away from the platform.

The four elements that Facebook prioritised in its new algorithm were:

- Links shared through Messenger.
- Comments or Likes.
- Multiple replies.
- Meaningful interactions, i.e. posts that create actual conversation between users.

These are the things you should definitely be doing more of.

Facebook inherently has a low rate of organic reach, in other words, the number of people who get to see your posts is small and posting anything relies heavily on other people liking and sharing it to gain momentum. You will notice that certain posts perform better than others. Personal photos work better than images taken from the internet, and a short personal video is better than a GIF from a movie or TV show. It could be that only 8% of your followers will see a post from you. It could also be that you are reaching the same small pool each time, in which case your posts might be entertaining to these followers, but not attracting any new purchases of your book.

You might be forgiven for wondering why you should even bother with Facebook at all if the realistic influence of it is so small as to be insignificant? Despite the manipulation of the algorithms to favour certain posts, and undoubtedly posts that are paid for advertising, Facebook still has the widest reach, and each of those users spends an average of an hour a day scrolling through their newsfeed picking up on all sorts of things.

Here are some ways you can help boost organic growth and can be applied to all social media:

- Post content that is visually attractive and interesting, and that will likely trigger an emotional response, (hence the plethora of kitten and puppy pictures). Short videos, no more than three minutes long, can generate 135% more reach than pictures alone. Video taken out 'in the wild' holds audience attention longer, and therefore gets picked up by the algorithms. Whatever you post it needs to be a scroll stopper.
- Post frequently, daily if possible. Get the algorithms interested in what's happening on your page. Mix it all up. Post stories, images with links, quotes, questions, polls, GIFS, video, and blog posts.
- Stay away from religion and politics unless that is crucial to your message.
- Always reply to audience comments or likes, immediately. Freshness counts.
- Don't be preoccupied with what you're selling, focus instead on the LGBTQ+ community, and especially your typical customer.
- Encourage comments by asking questions and creating debate. Always reply with an open-ended question to get the conversation flowing.

23.2 Facebook Advertising

Facebook will ask you all the time if you want to boost a post you've made on your author page. Paid for advertising can amount to ten times more engagement, but will that transpose into book sales? Some would say yes, but it's no good just putting in a few pounds here and there, you will need a sustained plan and that costs a good deal of money.

The principle behind using Facebook advertising is to utilise their algorithms and mega pool of data to place adverts aimed at people who are most likely to be interested in your book.

Millions of people use Facebook every day to keep up with friends, watch videos, hear breaking news stories, and occasionally some react to ads that pop up that they find interesting. But how realistic and worthwhile are the huge numbers of users when it comes to planting the idea of your book in a stranger's mind, and persuading them to buy it?

What are the advantages and the disadvantages of using Facebook ads?

Advantages:

- If you want to sell your book, the ideal is to have a pool of potential customers. Facebook, above anything else, provides that enormous online customer base, waiting to be tapped into. Even if all the people that you could reach do not want to buy your book, they might provide connections that could help expand your reach. People from all walks of life use Facebook.
- The greatest aspect of Facebook advertising is that it allows you to target the specific groups of people who will most likely be interested in your posts and

your book. Ads can be filtered by age, area, sexual orientation, gender, all sorts of things. You can be very specific or quite general, and the algorithms will tell you how wide an audience your ad is likely to reach.
- Facebook ads allow anyone with little or no marketing or advertising knowledge to start promoting their book and set the spend level to whatever suits their budget.
- As soon as someone likes, comments, or shares your ad, it appears on a percentage of their friends' newsfeeds, thus giving you increased exposure.
- It can push traffic towards your website. Adding a Facebook Pixel to your website pages will allow you to see who lands there and then clicks through to convert to a book purchase. And conversion measurement reporting, allows you to track the actions people take after viewing your ad.

Disadvantages:

- With so much happening every second on people's Facebook feeds it is extremely difficult to catch their attention. Strangers don't care about you or your book.
- There is so much information bombarding them from all the social media platforms, that to stand out in the crowd your ad has to be marketed very cleverly.
- One negative comment about your book or ad by a user can have an unfavourable effect. You are only as good as the last comment or review. Even if you address an issue quickly, you'll never know how many people might have seen a negative comment.
- Facebook ad marketing requires a lot of time and effort. If your energy levels and motivation are low,

the uphill struggle could be all-consuming. How much time and resources are you willing to devote to this aspect of your writing life?

- The amount you invest depends on your budget but be prepared to absorb negative remuneration.
- 'Post Boost' offers at £5 or £8 are unlikely to result in any worthwhile activity.
- A lot of Facebook advertising that pops up is considered by many to be nothing more than spam or worse still, a scam.
- The percentage of people who engage with a post or ad by liking, sharing, clicking, or commenting is shrinking year on year. Click-through rates are low.
- Younger social media users are moving away from Facebook, instead favouring Instagram, Snapchat, TikTok, and the like. If your target audience is older, this might not be an issue.
- Once someone likes your page this does not guarantee that they will see your posts in their news feed. People can unfollow at any time.

In short, it is not easy to measure success rates of Facebook ads absolutely. It might be that you will never know for sure the real impact you have with Facebook advertising. Success can only really be measured in the revenue produced. As long as you are not making losses, you might consider Facebook advertising to be successful.

23.3 Twitter

Tweets on Twitter are short statements and often political opinion that champions people's personal views to a wider, connected audience. Twitter is good for finding and nurturing beneficial relationships, even friendships, with like-minded people.

Setting up a Twitter account is straight forward. You can use whatever profile name you like, and Twitter will tell you if it has been used before. You can have one or as many accounts as you want, and you can link them to one Gmail or to different email addresses.

One tweet takes just 18 minutes to reach its full audience before it is buried in amongst the thousands of new tweets streaming into each individual newsfeed. Unless, and this is down to the magic and unpredictability of chaos, it happens to go viral, meaning it gets picked up and shared thousands, possibly millions of times. But even viral tweets are quickly forgotten.

As with Facebook, there are algorithms at play behind the scenes. You might notice that your tweets do not reach the number of people you expected, when other authors with similar numbers of followers, or even fewer, seem to get much better traction for seemingly posting the exact same 'writer lifting' tweets for example (a tweet that asks other writers to follow you with the promise that you'll reciprocate, thus increasing each profile's number of followers). It could be that you are following far more people compared to the number that are following you.

It seems that even if you only follow ten people, if 11 or 12 follow you back, that makes the algorithms work favourably towards you. The simple fact is that you need to get rid of people you are following who do not follow you back. Culling these unproductive followers can actually be quite therapeutic. The key is to get the ratio down to under one-to-one.

Contact the accounts you are interested in keeping, but who aren't following you back, (these will often be organisations), and put it to them that it would be of beneficial advantage to both of you if you follow each other. Tailor a personal message to each one. With this nudge, you will find at least some will follow you back. Of the remaining ones, unfollow them. Unless you are interested in what they tweet about, because without following you back, they will not see your tweets and therefore will never 'like' or 'share' them.

Most LGBTQ+ organisations have a Twitter account. If you can't find it immediately on Twitter itself, search for them online. Social media links are usually located as an icon at the bottom of the home-page. Follow as many other LGBTQ+ writers, professionals, and anyone else you think could influence your future readers, but each month have a look at those you followed and who didn't follow back, and decide if you are interested enough to keep them. For people looking at your Twitter page, if your follow ratio is in your favour, it suggests that your brand is a positive one.

Another thing you can do to increase your follower numbers, is to look for LGBTQ+ authors who have used the hashtag #writerslift or #promolgbtq or any other hashtags relevant to you. Put the hashtag into the search bar and a long list of authors and creatives will come up. Scroll through and follow the ones you like the look of. Keep a list and wait to see which ones follow you back. Some will, some won't, that's fine. You will find that within a few days these different strategies will gain you many more followers than you would have by doing nothing. Asking for followers is not shameful, and it makes perfect sense for both parties involved when the idea is to increase follower numbers. The more followers you have, the wider your tweets will travel.

The difference between the interface of Twitter and Facebook, is that Facebook is built on social groups, like family, friendship circles and discovering your tribes. Twitter is more about the individual speaking: it is more political, opinion driven, and slightly edgier.

- The best time to Tweet is between 5pm and 8pm when people are on their way home from work.
- Tweets with images receive 18% more click-throughs to book selling platforms.
- Tweets with images receive 89% more likes and 150% more retweets.
- Tweets with just one hashtag are 69% more likely to be retweeted.
- 92% of companies tweet more than once a day.

Use Twitter to ask questions around relevant hashtags to your subject or do a poll: 'Do you know the difference between gender and sexuality? #gender #sexuality #LGBTQ'. How many people respond? What gender are they; what age? Follow them and interact with them. If you're writing a blog on the back of this information, quote some of those Tweets, and include their account names and keywords used. You will find, through experience, how best to pitch your posts, but always aim to be interesting and interested in others.

Remember, 500 million tweets are sent out each day. That's something like 6,000 per second. It is a fast moving, scrolling screen, so do not be disheartened that your tweets only appear to reach a handful of people who respond with a like. You will get to learn what works best for you and you can click on your tweet activity to get a detailed picture of how widely your tweets are being read and interacted with.

'Impressions' means that your tweet has been delivered to that many timelines (different user accounts). It doesn't guarantee that all of them will have read it, just that they might have done, and it can give you an idea of the potential size of any given conversation. 'Total Engagements' means the total number of times users interacted with a tweet, i.e. they clicked somewhere on the tweet, either by retweeting (which is the ideal), replied to the tweet, or liked it (both also good).

23.4 Hashtags – What Are They And How To Use Them?

A hashtag can be one word, or a string of words preceded by # (the hash sign). It identifies a keyword or phrase on a topic of interest to allow people to search for it. As soon as you use a hashtag in a post or tweet, it is indexed and then made available to be seen by anyone who searches for that hashtag. You can invent your own hashtags, especially for your book title, and use them whenever you like. Remember, a hashtag only works if other people are using it.

Hashtags help to narrow down topics and subjects that are of interest. For instance, someone who wants the latest news or stories about a TV programme would search # followed by the name of that programme or news item. This applies to everything and anything you can think of.

When searching for a hashtag on your social media, you are directed to a page that combines all the posts using that hashtag in real time order. If a keyword hashtag gains enough clicks and momentum, it can start to 'trend', which means it is being searched for by a significant number of users. You don't always want to use the most popular hashtags because your post will simply move down the list so quickly it will only be seen by a few people if you're lucky. Commonly used or trending hashtags will have a number attached to them in thousands of users.

Always try to use one or two relevant hashtags when you're writing a post and hashtags with ten or more characters receive better engagement than shorter ones. Research by TrackMaven has shown that when posts contain more than two hashtags there is a significant decline in participation by viewers. On Instagram, however, the story is different. It appears that nine or ten hashtags is the optimum number. Generally, posts with hashtags are twice as likely to engage and get 55% more retweets (a retweet is sending a tweet forward with a new comment attached or simply the original tweet).

If you're unsure which hashtag is best to use, there are a number of sites where you can pay for comprehensive hashtag data. However, with a little exploration around the internet you can easily find what you're looking for. Just type in 'top LGBTQ+ hashtags' and you'll get the information you require. Look through other people's streams who are posting on similar topics to see which hashtags they use.

The hashtag #OTD (on this day) is good when considering LGBTQ+ history. Daily hashtags or #tbt (throwback Thursday for instance), are a good way to keep you posting each day but use them in a relevant way. Use any hashtags that relate to your book and LGBTQ+ topic.

Also include the @ addresses in your posts of one or more allies, organisations and institutes aligned with your topic. This will ensure that they see your post and will hopefully react to it.

23.5 Copyright

Some people worry that their social media posts can be used by anyone. The simple answer is that you are protected. There are criteria though: the content must be original, and must possess a minimal amount of creativity. A list of facts, therefore, would not be protected. It must also contain more than just a name, a single word, or short phrase. Any ideas your tweets or posts formulate are not covered under copyright, only the exact wording you use.

Twitter states in its terms and conditions, (check for up to date Ts & Cs), that you retain your rights to any content you submit, including your personal photos. However, you also grant Twitter a licence to use the content which authorises them to make your posts available to the rest of the world. This enables other users the licence to copy and retweet your posts. That, of course, is the social aspect and ethos behind social media platforms like Twitter, and our desire to share interesting content that appeals to others.

Taking your tweets and using them elsewhere breaches the copyright laws. But, if someone copies your tweet by embedding it into their website for instance, it is still technically a retweet because the site has used Twitter's own tools to display it fully with your profile picture and username. If you want to stop this happening you need to make your account private, meaning that only your chosen, and presumably trusted followers, can see your content. The alternative is to delete the post.

23.6 Other Social Media

Do plenty of research into the different social media platforms there are before you get started on building your author profile. New ones come along and fill specific needs, especially for younger markets, with increasing regularity, and there will no doubt be others in the future too.

If you already have a Facebook account, that's a pretty good place to start because of its familiarity, plus you can push your friends towards your new author page.

All the major social media networks have millions, some even billions, of users. While Facebook has over two billion monthly active users, platforms such as Pinterest, though much smaller in its number of user accounts, still has 250 million. The differences between the social media networks, in terms of their reach, is virtually irrelevant when considering such huge numbers as these, unless you are a large multinational company.

You will never get to reach everyone on social media, no matter how many platforms you are on or how active you are, the numbers are just too great.

Here is some information about some of the other popular social media platforms to help you decide which ones are right for you:

YouTube

YouTube is a platform that allows you to upload videos. It appeals to all ages, and 62% of its users are male.

How far you go in producing, or having produced for you, a book promo video is entirely up to you and your budget, but you can record your own videos on your phone, then edit, insert music and add captions. Social media algorithms are always more favourable towards personally made videos.

Setting up a YouTube Channel is straightforward, and many authors use it to host their vlogs, interviews, or tutorials. In fact, any video material that relates to you, your research, or your book can be uploaded to make a library of video content. Always cross-promote through your other social media pages to draw traffic to your YouTube channel to boost its ranking.

Instagram

This social media platform is most popular with those in the age bracket 18 to 29, and 68% of its users are female. It is about the instant sharing of images and videos from mobile phones. This might be good for you if your book has the potential to be visual, as it allows you to be creative with your picture taking and image ideas.

Linkedin

Users of Linkedin are fairly evenly split between male and female, and predominantly in the 25- to 54-year-old age group. Professionals use it to connect with each other, so it is an ideal place to show off your expertise, promote your credentials, relevant qualifications, experience and anything you've been involved in with the LGBTQ+ community.

Use Linkedin to become a recognised voice on topics and LGBTQ+ issues that are important to you. Here you can write, and post longer articles and features with pictures. Use it much like a blog. It is good for connecting with other writers and influencers in the LGBTQ+ community.

Pinterest

The average age of Pinterest users is 40 and 80% are female. This social media is image based, like an online scrapbook, and great for building storyboards of evocative images. Businesses post prodigiously every day, but you can build-up your storyboards over time. It is good for driving traffic towards your book.

Goodreads

Goodreads is the site for book lovers, readers and writers, and where users review books. There are over 450 LGBTQ+ groups on Goodreads, who talk about new releases and old favourites in groups that cover a wide range of sub-genres. It is a good place for networking and finding like-minded authors.

Whichever social media platforms you choose to use, stick to those, and work at building up your followers on each. Deciding on one or two you are sure you can manage regularly is perfectly sufficient. Anymore and you might suffer the stress of not reaching your follower targets, not posting regularly enough, not being witty, intelligent or spontaneous, all things that will only lead to increased pressure on you to maintain them. One day you might get to the stage where you need, and can afford help, but to begin with, keep things manageable. Learn as you go, what works, and what doesn't work, for you.

Social media is a marvel of our time and its benefits are huge, but it also has a dark side. For many LGBTQ+ people, discrimination and disapproval, even sometimes hostility, are sadly well-known. Mostly, we manage to overcome it, and we should always do so with dignity. Brush disapprovers aside, forget them, and move on.

Be confident, and portray the image of the author you want to be.

24. Telling *their* Story: Ian Elmslie

Ian is a gay man and lives in London. He used to play keyboard in a duo called *Katrina and the Boy* in the eighties and early nineties. They were well-known on the gay cabaret circuit and toured with Lily Savage, and were regulars at the famous London gay venue, the Royal Vauxhall Tavern. During those years, Ian bumped into and met many big-name celebrities; Cilla Black, Donny Osmond, David Bowie, to name but a few.

When *Katrina and the Boy* disbanded, Ian went into teaching. He never set out to write a book, and certainly didn't want to write one that was a tittle-tattle gossip exposé of the stars he'd met and happened to catch off guard in his cabaret days.

I asked Ian, what was his motivation for writing his book *A Marvellous Party*?

I have always been an open book – ha ha, no pun intended, but all these stories, I had shared before with close friends, and even therapists. It wasn't by any means a sense of unburdening myself, more that I was completing a part of a journey. It felt more like sharing, rather than offloading. An encouragement to other people to consider their journey, their heroes, their life's achievements, and their hopes for the next part of their lives. I'd lost my brother in the most tragic of circumstances, and I'd left a job I loved before my set intention, due to disappointing changes in education. Although I had reconciled myself with the loss of my sibling, and was almost relieved to leave teaching, I had no idea what I was going to do next.

Then, a week after my last day at school, Cilla Black died. I'd been at a party where she was a guest a mere six weeks previous, and I wrote a short tribute to her that I shared on my Facebook page. The response was so encouraging that I decided to write more tales of brief encounters with celebrities, with the aim of posting a new story every Saturday. It was only when I realised that I wasn't writing 'ticklish gossip', but a reflection on the important influence of these extraordinary men and women, did I realise that I was writing a book. The fiftieth anniversary of the partial decriminalisation of homosexuality was the final piece of the puzzle. Thus, it became an historical reflection on my experiences since 1967, and those who had guided me along the road. But I never intended to write a book, and I remain amazed to this day that I did. It was never on my list of things to do, but I am enormously proud of the achievement. So many people say, 'I should write a book', don't they, but they never do. I think everyone should. If you get to 50 and haven't got a story to tell, either ask for your money back or get busy!

Is there anything you wish you'd left out or perhaps added?

Editing is the writer's best friend, and worst enemy. I liken it to cutting the curls off your baby. You know it's time for a 'big boy's haircut', but he's so cute. Editing hurts. You've poured everything onto the page, and you've worked so hard. But some of it has to go. I remember working with my publisher on the first chapter, and I just couldn't seem to please him. I thought I'd never get it right. Then he said, 'remember, we've promised them funny stories about meeting heroes.' It was that simple. I cut the first 26 pages. When I knew what would make the book better, I was off; cut, cut, cut. Or, as Stephen King advises, 'Omit unnecessary words!'

I am never satisfied with my work. When I do readings, I'm still snipping words and sentences. The baby still has some curls, but he wears them well.

On the day of publication, my wonderful publisher said to me, 'You know what this book is about, don't you?'

I responded with one word, 'Heroes.'

He smiled, and said, 'Yes, but it's also about survival.'

I'd never thought of that, but he was dead right, as he always is. It's about how I got from who and where I was, to who and where and what I needed to be. Out of the darkness into the light, guided by a song on the radio, a TV show, a book, a film. The breadcrumbs that lead us out of the woods.

Ian Elmslie's book *A Marvellous Party* is available through www.ignitebooks.co.uk Ian can be found on Twitter @ianelmslie62 on Facebook @ianelmslie and on Instagram @amarvellousparty

25. Frequently Asked Questions

In this chapter I answer some of the questions I often get asked about writing and self-publishing.

Can you recommend an editor and/or proof reader?

I would love to recommend my own editor of *How to: Tell Your LGBTQ+ Story*. I'm sure Nick Taylor would work well with you, but it is essential that you do your own research to find a suitable editor or proof reader for you. Someone you can work with, who understands your topic and genre, and what you are trying to say through your work. When you do find the right one you should hang onto them.

As mentioned previously in this book, (See sub-chapter: 5.1 Planning Your Budget), there is an online group called The Alliance of Independent Authors (ALLi), which has a database including editors and proof readers. It is a subscription-based service, but it does offer help and support, and lists people with expertise in all sorts of areas to do with publishing.

All such services come at a cost, but with due diligence and investigation you should find someone who fits your remit. I wouldn't go down the route of using someone from a site like Fiverr for instance, without proper, verifiable recommendations. Try researching similar books to the one you want to write, find out the names of the editors and Google them. Look as well at professional organisations like the Chartered Institute of Editing and Proofreading (CIEP).

With regards to proof readers: there are very few books, even traditionally published, that do not contain one single typo or other error, but readers will not forgive page after page of misspellings, grammatical mishaps, and factual inaccuracies. Before you let anyone see your manuscript you must check and double-check yourself every single word you've written, and you will probably do this a dozen times or more. (See chapter: 11. Editors, Editing, and Proofreading).

What are the benefits of using a 'publishing company'?

When you say 'publishing company' do you mean a traditional publisher, vanity publisher, or partnership publishing company? When referring to a traditional publishing house, the onus is with them using you, not the other way around. They are the ones who choose to take you on, or not. You decide whether to sign a contract and work with them, but only if they believe you are worth investing in. The advantage of scooping a publishing deal with a traditional publisher is the distribution such companies can bring. (See sub-chapter: 2.2 Book Distribution).

If, on the other hand, you are referring to a publisher who you pay for their services to get your book published, such as a vanity publisher or partnership publisher, the costs involved can be significant, but with editorial, formatting, cover design, and some distribution in the package, this can be a way forward if you really do not want that responsibility yourself. (See sub-chapter: 2.1 Partnership Publishing).

How realistic is it that I could find a publisher who would take me on?

To be honest, pretty unrealistic. The LGBTQ+ market is small. About 3% of Kindle e-books are categorised as LGBTQ+, according to research by K-lytics. While that still amounts to a large section of the whole market value, in the eyes of publishers, it is small and not nearly lucrative enough and therefore worth them investing in. Sub-genres within the LGBTQ+ category are consequently very niche indeed. Publishers spend huge sums of money on their chosen authors and must recoup that outlay and make a profit. Add to this the fact that most publishers will not even look at an unsolicited manuscript without it first being forwarded to them by an agent, and you might as well be on a road to nowhere.

Publishers and agents are inundated with manuscripts every day, and they spend a lot of their expertise and time working with just a few of these authors whom they know will make them significant sales. Really, before thinking about a publisher, you need to get an agent, if that is the route you want to take. You will find that process too will take a long time, and may never happen, because, as with publishers, agents will only take on clients they think will make them money. (See chapter: 2. Publishers and Agents).

The purpose of my book is to reach a family member I have not spoken to in years but also to tell my story to a wider public. Is this a good idea?

Many authors, throughout history, have used their books as a means of connecting with someone; to tell them something they cannot articulate in a conversation or within the constraints of a letter or because time and circumstance has not made this possible. It would be preferrable to confess in person, of course, but that is not always easy for many reasons. You could include the dilemma of this situation in your story: how you hadn't spoken for many years to this person, then met and told them about wanting to write your book, and the consequences of that on your relationship with them.

Always think very carefully about the different outcomes and the effect your book might have on other people and especially those close to you. You want your story to reach other people in similar situations, and indeed a wider audience, but don't write it for them. Think about what is already out there on the market. Every story is individual, but what we long for in other people's stories, when we are looking for support, is similarity. Seeing our LGBTQ+ selves represented in society gives us strength and support. Concentrate on the book being about you and your story and it will reach its target audience by default because they will be searching for just such a book.

Will using a penname and remaining anonymous have a negative impact?

I cannot visualise any negative impact from using a penname. Only, possibly, that people might assume you are 'hiding' your identity. But if you are, it is for a very good reason. Be open about your reasons for using a penname if asked and that should be enough to allay any suspicions. Personally, I have not found a downside to using a penname, only in that it can get a bit confusing sometimes when people know me as one name and forget that I'm David when I'm doing interviews. (See sub-chapter: 1.2 Using a Penname).

When can I call myself a professional writer/author?

'Professional' inherently means something that is your occupation and that you earn a living from, but the title of writer or author can be assumed by anyone, and legitimately so by those who do in fact write.

In the old days, before the internet, to be an author of a book invariably meant that you were published in the traditional way; a vocation that was open to very few people. The 'right of entry' to this world was restrictive and subsequently deemed elitist. Thus, being an author or writer came with perceived ideas about what it meant to achieve that. The question is when does that phrase of 'I am a writer/author', become earned? Is it when you first have an article published in a magazine, or is it something more substantial like self-publishing a book? Is it when people approach you for guidance or your 'expert opinion'? Or is it when your book sales are sufficient that you can make a reasonable living? The answer is that it doesn't matter. Naming your trade, that of writer or author, does not mean that you ally yourself to a particular image someone else has of what that is. The truth is, if you want to call yourself a writer or author or LGBTQ+ activist, do so. It is your goals, dreams and aspirations that matter, not other people's perceptions – they are fleeting and momentary.

I want to aim my book at a wide age range, from teenagers to pensioners. Is this realistic?

Don't aim it at any single age group, unless you are writing on a topic that is peculiar to a specific age. Writing for children and young adults is a skill itself. Your book will slot into the right place through your writing. It might be generation biased because it is you writing it, but hopefully it will resonate with a much wider audience. Try to stick to what you know you can achieve.

Once your book is written you will be able to identify your typical customer, but don't narrow your appeal before you've written it. (See sub-chapter: 16.4 Defining Your Typical Customer).

What do you wish you'd known before you started writing your books?

I wrote a couple of novels which were not selling. If I'd realised sooner that so many opportunities would be made available to me through writing LGBTQ+ non-fiction, I would have done that years earlier. But perhaps I had to learn that for myself.

Are there any things that could catch me out that I might not even be aware of?

No end of things! You are on a journey and you will find out the pitfalls and advantages in your own time. Any advantage you have discovered for yourself is hugely gratifying, and yet it might not be seen as such by the next person. In life we make mistakes and we learn from the things that do work for us.

Write your book, get it edited and proofread, and then the fun begins. The most important thing to be aware of is to only invest in your book what you can afford to lose. Tell yourself that you are not going to make a fortune, but that you can hope to at least cover your costs, meet some interesting people, and do some fun things you never thought would happen to you. (See sub-chapter: 5.1 Planning Your Budget).

Do you have any tips when it comes to using social media?

Facebook can be challenging because posts are only ever seen by a handful of people through organic reach (unless you pay for advertising). It is good for finding and joining groups and keeping your local community updated on what you're doing, especially if you're thinking about a book launch in your town. Twitter is good for building brand awareness.

One thing, as we all know, social media can be exhausting and sometimes demoralising, and there is a certain amount of risk of being targeted by 'trolls' or people making unkind comments. Never post or join in with any negativity, even if you agree with the argument, and absolutely never interact with bad comments made about your tweets or posts. (See chapter: 23. Social Media).

Should I use a particular punctuation style, for instance use single, or double speech marks?

I would say always use Times New Roman typeface size 11pt, unless you are writing for children or have a very good reason to do otherwise. That is what most people are used to seeing in books. Typically, double speech marks are an American preference, usually in English we use single speech marks. If it helps, have a style sheet (see Nick Taylor's style sheet at JustWriteRight.co.uk). (See chapter: 14. Formatting And Uploading Your Book).

Do you self-edit?

Yes. Lots. Continually. Here is my writing process: First, I write. This sounds obvious, but it is the main thing you need to do, and no editing of any sort can take place until you've written something. I start with some basic ideas for chapters (I'm talking non-fiction here), just a chapter heading, and maybe a paragraph or two – the essence of what I want the chapter to be about. Once I have an idea for the overall structure of the book, what I want to say, and what I want people to take away from it, I then start writing around what I've outlined. Over time the semblance of a manuscript starts to come together. I treat this as my first rough WIP (work in progress) and go back to the beginning to start shaping, cutting, and editing as I progress forward.

At the end of that, I go back again and begin editing properly to a standard that I am happy with. It is not ready for publication yet, but I am happy to let someone else look at it at this stage. This is when I get my editor involved. After editing, I do a read-through in the book format template so that I can see how it will look on the page and send a couple of chapters at a time to my proof reader. As the chapters come back from my proof reader I amend any typos, sentence restructure, grammar or overall structural suggestions. I then read-through at least twice more to do any final tweaks.

In answer to the question, a lot of the discipline of writing comes down to an awful lot of self-editing, but the professional edit should be paid for, and carried out by someone who has the expertise. Also, they are emotionally detached from the work; this is an important aspect of editing. (See chapter: 11. Editors, Editing And Proofreading).

How do I copyright my work?

If someone steals your words you could, in theory, sue them. New writers often excessively worry about this, but the likelihood of it happening is so remote as to make it almost irrelevant. It is more likely to happen to a best-selling established author.

Once you have formatted your manuscript and uploaded it to your chosen digital platform or passed it to the publishing company, your work is copyrighted, and no one can steal it as their own or plagiarise it. If you are concerned about sending your manuscript out to editors and proof readers before it is published, put the copyright sign on each page with your name and book title. There is a standard copyright text which appears at the front of all books. Copy that into your own book (changing the name and dates). Also, every book has a unique ISBN.

According to the GOV.UK website, 'You automatically get copyright protection when you create: original literary, dramatic, musical and artistic work, including illustration and photography, and original non-literary written work such as software, web content and databases.'

Is there anything I need to do regarding copyrighting a penname?

I use a penname, that is my penname, and no one else can use it to pretend to be me, just as no one can fraudulently use my real name either. Of course, there may be hundreds of people in the world with the same name (you only need look at Facebook to find that out), but they cannot pretend to be you. Basically, if you can prove that an original piece of work is yours, the law is on your side (see previous question on copyright).

If you do have a common name, you might consider using another or just your initials to stop any confusion with someone else. (See sub-chapter: 1.2 Using A Penname).

What programme do you use to write your books in?

I simply use Word, the thesaurus button and the Concise Oxford Dictionary. There is no hidden magic in writing that can be aided through software other than the organisation of files. There are subscription packages, like Scrivener, developed specifically for authors to do this.

How do you find someone to do your book cover art?

For self-published authors, the cover art and design of their book is a very important and personal thing. It is the embodiment of the vision of how they dream their book should look. Traditionally published authors do not have this luxury and relinquish that responsibility to the publisher's own design team.

If your desire is to have a beautiful bespoke piece of art as the focus of your book cover, get a professional artist to do it rather than have a go at it yourself, and don't employ somebody just because they're arty. Then hand the work of designing the cover including that artwork, over to a book cover designer. Remember, art is a very personal thing and what you might think speaks volumes about your LGBTQ+ topic might leave the next person stone cold.

I would suggest avoiding using arty images that grate against other book cover designs in your genre. Look at those books and make a list of the designers you admire and Google them. Do your research to find one you like, trust, and can afford. If the designer is any good, they will come up with something that meets your brief, does not juxtapose with similar themed books but which will also stand out on the shelf. (See chapter: 13. Cover Design).

Epilogue

My purpose in writing this book has been to show people from the LGBTQ+ community, firstly the importance of telling and sharing our stories, and secondly, how to achieve that and reach an audience.

Each past generation of LGBTQ+ young people has had to find the answers to all their questions with little if any prominent historical documentation or representation of themselves in popular culture to draw upon. The unique ability our generation has, is being able to pass on our knowledge and experience of living our LGBTQ+ lives, and that cannot be overstated.

If our stories reach one other person and help them to realise that they are not the only one in the world to feel the way they do, then surely it is worth the effort of writing and publishing them. With this mind, I very much hope that you have found some inspiration from the other writers who have talked about their own writing and coming out journeys in this book. I hope too, that the information and encouragement provided in these pages gives you the inspiration to write about your own journeys and tell *your* LGBTQ+ story. Please do let me know how that goes for you.

Coming out is not resolved on one day or one occasion. For me, that journey is still on going, and with each book I write, so another perspective to my understanding of my coming out story is revealed to me, and crucially, what my place in the world is. It is a continuing process and an enjoyable one. It is always cathartic, and writing this book has been no exception.

Being true to ourselves is an immensely strong human desire and it is just as important no matter where you live in the world. None of us are so vastly different, despite our backgrounds, upbringing, culture or ethnicity. Whether we live in London, Chennai or Los Angeles, we all yearn for the same basic need – to be who we are.

It has been my huge privilege to talk to so many interesting and inspiring LGBTQ+ writers who were willing to share their own experiences of telling their stories. It was a pleasure and a revelation. Like me, they all felt they were alone in struggling with their feelings, and every one of them had been desperate to read other people's stories that spoke to them; that they could relate to and identify with. By not telling their stories, they knew they would be leaving other LGBTQ+ people abandoned in the same way they had been.

The need for community and the reaching hand of friendship has never been more apparent or needed as it has been during this time of the Corona Virus Pandemic. Isolation and loneliness have been particularly acute for those already on the margins of society, largely forgotten, and that of course includes many LGBTQ+ people. What this period of enforced exclusion has allowed for however, is the time to re-evaluate our lives and where we see our futures. We have been given time to think about what is really important to us.

I believe that this period, especially in LGBTQ+ history, will see an abundance of creative outpouring from those who have been stuck at home. What better time to write that book about your LGBTQ+ life experiences than now?

If you ask the question, 'Where are the LGBTQ+ people that represent me; that mirror who I am?'

The answer is clear: Here we are!

~

Helpful Links

Category Is Bookshop www.categoryisbooks.com An independent LGBTQIA+ bookshop in Glasgow.
Diva www.divamag.co.uk Monthly lesbian life and culture magazine.
Encompass Network www.encompassnetwork.org.uk Run an annual LGBTQ+ creative writing competition sponsored by Cambridge University Press.
Erotic Review www.eroticreviewmagazine.com Subscription only monthly magazine for sophisticated erotic lifestyle and fiction e-zine.
Gay Authors Workshop www.gayauthorsworkshop.uk For a small annual subscription, Gay Authors Workshop offers an association of LGBTQ+ poets, dramatists, fiction and non-fiction writers, a supportive forum to discuss and develop their work.
Gay's The Word www.gaystheword.co.uk The UK's oldest LGBTQ+ bookshop and touchstone for the broader LGBTQ+ community.
Gay Times www.gaytimes.co.uk Gay current affairs, opinion, culture, art and style, articles and interviews.
Imaan @ImaanLGBTQ on Twitter Imaan supports Muslim people, their families and friends, to address issues of sexual orientation within Islam.
Lambda Literary Awards www.LAMBDALiterary.org For over 30 years Lambda has championed LGBTQ+ books.
Meetup www.meetup.com Sign up for free and search for writers, book or other relevant groups. Or start your own group.
Out On The Page www.outonthepage.co.uk An Arts Council Funded Project to support LGBTQ+ writers, including workshops and writing retreats.

Outstanding Stories www.outstandingstories.net Australia's premier LGBTQ+ creative writing competition.

Pink News www.pinknews.co.uk Online newspaper for lesbians and gay men.

Polari Prize www.polarisalon.com The UK's only book awards for emerging and established LGBTQ+ writers.

The Portal Bookshop https://the-portal-bookshop.sqaure.site LGBTQIA books sourced from the UK and beyond.

QueerLit www.queerlit.co.uk An online queer literature book selling service.

Queer Indie https://queerindie.com/ A group of cross-genre authors writing queer/ally books.

Rainbow Dads Podcast https://rbd2019.podbean.com/ A series in which five gay and bi men tell their stories about coming out in heterosexual marriages.

Sarbat www.sarbat.net A support and social group for LGBT Sikhs.

Stonewall www.stonewall.org.uk A lesbian, gay, bisexual and transgender rights charity in the UK.

Terence Higgins Trust www.tht.org.uk A British charity that campaigns on various issues related to AIDS and HIV.

Acknowledgements

I must thank all the writers who gave their time freely to be part of this book. Without their voices it would have been very a different and less inspiring 'how-to' guide.

Thank you:

Curtis Chin
Helen Dale
Frederic Davies
Ian Elmslie
Gireesh
JD Glass

Hugo Greenhalgh
Cameron D. James
Gary H. James
Nick Taylor
Gideon E. Wood

My immense gratitude also to Nick Taylor www.justwriteright.co.uk for his editorial skills, and to Jan Ellison for her proofreading, and the great cover design by Garrett Leigh www.blackjazzdesign.com

If you have been inspired by *How to: Tell Your LGBTQ+ Story*, please use the link below to leave a review. A simple kind word or two might be all it takes to encourage another LGBTQ+ person to tell *their* story too.

www.amazon.co.uk/howtotellyourlgbtq+story/createreview

I'd love to hear from you about your publishing experiences. You can find me @davidledain on Twitter and Facebook, and on the Rainbow Dads Podcast @rainbowdads on Twitter and Instagram.

Thank you, David.

www.ingramcontent.com/pod-product-compliance
Lightning Source LLC
Chambersburg PA
CBHW052019070526
44584CB00016B/1819